THE WORLD IS *NOT* YOUR OYSTER!

THE WORLD IS *NOT* YOUR OYSTER!

AMERICA: THE LOST EMPIRE

BERNARD BALL

BRIDGET MCCOY

Outskirts Press, Inc.
Denver, Colorado

Outskirts Press, Inc.
http://www.outskirtspress.com

ISBN: 978-1-4327-5083-1

Outskirts Press and the "OP" logo are trademarks belonging to Outskirts Press, Inc.

PRINTED IN THE UNITED STATES OF AMERICA

"No matter what country or continent we come from, we are basically the same human beings. We have the common human needs and concerns. We all seek happiness and try to avoid suffering regardless of our race, religion, sex, or political status . . . The rich diversity of cultures and religions should help to strengthen the fundamental human rights in all communities. Because underlying this diversity are fundamental principles that bind us as members of the same human family. . . . It is not only our right as members of the global human family to protest when our brothers and sisters are being treated brutally, but it is also our duty to do whatever we can to help them."

The Dalai Lama

This book is dedicated to the children of Haiti, Rwanda, Ethiopia, Sudan and Somalia. A portion of the proceeds from the sales of this book will be donated to improve the quality of life for these children.

Acknowledgements

This book is dedicated to all those who provided inspiration and displayed patience while awaiting this publication, as well as those who inspired me to write other books.

To my mother, Odessa Olga Williams, aka Thelma Argo Ball, I would not be here were it not for you. You always stressed that education, dedication and commitment would get you wherever you wanted to be. Truly, it has been through self-education and all my other successful endeavors that have brought me to this letter-writing campaign of all letter-writing campaigns.

To Bridget, my friend and confidante, who has truly been an inspiration like no other. This is not the first book she has co-authored. She is an educator in the truest sense of the word, a splendid editor and virtual assistant (Foster Business Solutions). I can't say enough about how much your support has meant, with this endeavor and with keeping my other businesses on track.

To Ellen Jackson (RIP Bria), a beautiful friend and poet; Brandon, now a twelve-year-old future renaissance man who spent many hours entertaining himself while we labored to finish this book; Treyvon Brommell…listen to your mother Shri (we call her Shira); and Shri, you listen to your mother Betty Sanders.

Marlana, Marques, and Marlon, I love ya'll. Marques, you're the royalty; remember the things you and I learned along the way. Marlana, someday we'll meet again; Marlon I am very proud of you and think you will someday make an imprint on how history is taught.

Victoria Stewart, aka Tori aka Deena, you're the epitome of what America should be. Remember the late nights working the rehab and congratulations on the birth of your granddaughter; extend my congratulations to Rob and Aaron, too.

To my sister Valorie Maria Ball Allen: cut the cake. I'll see you soon, Nikki and Rhonda. Blake, remember life is the beginning to a path of travel and death is the end of that journey; travel the right path and never look back.

For my sister, Sylvia Livingston, who is a great writer: I hope you take heed and get your book published!

My brothers Robert (Bobby), William (Kenny), Timothy (Tim), and David, I love you guys more than you will ever know. Hold on to your swagger and keep on being good fathers to your children as long as they will have you and someday, life will give you a return on your investment.

My baby sister Cheryl and her husband Michael gave birth to two of the finest boys in this world, Michael, Jr. and Mikael Harris, who will grow up to be two fine young men with promising futures. Uncle Bernie loves you guys.

Prodigal sister Jacquelyn, you should call sometime... Congratulations Dee on your insurance company; you should get back to singing.

Debbie (my sister and former running buddy) and Elwood Freeman, you both have also been an inspiration.

To my father who died October 9....I never say the year because that is how I keep him near.

Thanks to photographer Michael Whitehead and graphic designer Joey Wilson (Loud Designs), for the time spent in trying to develop a cover photo that would capture the essence of the book.

Karla Hufford, Guatemalan Beauty and photographer extraordinaire, is credited with the photo composition that graces the cover of this book. Thank you!

To Jose Yepez and his beautiful wife, a very special lady, congratulations on the birth of your daughter. You're a helluva guy.

Michele Longboat and her mother Lee, aka Squirrel, continue to give each other that kind of support, and Squirrel hope you find this book as interesting as you said it would be.

Sam Perez you're a helluva guy, a great father and professional mobile mechanic. Remember our countless debates and keep your political savvy.

John Caylor thanks for the fun we had riding our motorcycles. Tiffany and Sean look after your dad. Linda Wolfe you recommended a great book keep up your reading. Wendell Vaught, Master Naturalist, now that the book is finished, I can take you up on the EcoTour of the Everglades.

James and Gloria Suydam, it's been wonderful getting to know you guys and hanging out. I love you both. Can't wait to see that restored VW!

Tim Harding thanks for the support you showed for Bay Area Academy and for being a great neighbor!

Preface

Throughout the writing of this book, there were many transitions that took place that impacted and even slowed its development. We were involved in several major endeavors that were negatively affected by the downfall of the economy, from our real estate investments to Bay Area Academy (Laura Johnson, we ain't done yet!). We dealt with health issues, burglary of the first manuscript and the disappearance of my retirement fund when the hedge funds went belly up with the rest of the economy. But the band played on!

I think America is the greatest country in the world and I live in it, so I feel it is my duty to say what I think, especially since I believe it will save this country from G_D's wrath if taken to heart. Hopefully when this book is finished, it will be put on the shelves and into the hands of every person, rich or poor, young or old, black or white, believer or non-believer, not just here in America, but all over the world.

It is my hope that this book will deliver a message that will awaken the people's minds, provoke thought and incite action to bring about change. There are those, including myself, who want real change in this country; who don't want the government to have so much control over the working middle class that it is reduced to the underclass... everything this country does here or abroad, is motivated by the dollar, based on deceit and oppression and determined by race and class, instead of what is right and acceptable in the eyes of our creator. America is on a serious moral decline from which it may never recover. This book was not written under the premise that this is a problem for the black race or the white race but for the human race. However, we do have to acknowledge the burden the white man bears for being held responsible for the ills of this country, past and present. We are suppose to live and abide by the constitution of the United States, but there is some confusion there, because in the original version there was nothing that addressed the black man or the woman, black or white, so I guess black men and women of all races can do as they damn well please...so ladies give'em hell until they (the powers that be) do.

Readers are invited to independently confirm or refute the evidence presented within....for a discussion of the issues addressed in this book, visit my blog at www.tetrahedron.wordpress.com.

Contents

CHAPTER 1

The Lost Empire Begins At Home

America may consider itself a great nation, but as history has taught us, all great nations rise and fall, eventually becoming nothing more than artifacts in a museum or stories in the history books, and America is no exception. Some experience a gradual moral decline, like America is right now, and others fall at the hands of conquerors.

Consider some of the great empires of the past... from Biblical times to the 20th century, we've seen the rise and fall of the great Babylonian Empire of the Middle East under Nebuchadnezzar, the mighty Roman Empire which once ruled the earth, the Third Reich of Germany, the imperialist British Empire, and most recently, the Union of the Soviet Socialist Republic, a superpower whose reach covered an area two and a half times that of the United States. Some of these, like the Babylonian and Roman Empires, fell due to moral decay, while the others fell by the conquest of the people. America's decline most closely resembles that of the Roman Empire.

America's fall will be the result of its slide down the slippery slope of moral decay. What was once held sacred and revered, is now rejected and the attitude of America is every man for himself...if it makes you feel good, do it; never mind if you cause pain for someone else while creating pleasure for yourself.

There are many signs of America's moral decline. Turn on the radio and you'll hear profanity that should make you cringe but it is accepted as the norm. The music is full of graphic sex...nothing is left to the imagination! Hell, I remember back in the 80's seeing a sitcom that Whitney Houston was guest starring in and she had to change the lyrics of her song from "making love the whole night through" to "holding hands the whole night through"! Today, she could sing about sucking her man's d**k and wouldn't have to change a word (see what I mean!).

Used to be a time when the censors would bleep out the profanity but not anymore. Now, the record companies make two versions of a song, the "clean" version and the uncensored version; all they have to do is stick a warning label on the cover and they're free to record whatever they want. It then becomes incumbent upon the parents to monitor what their children are buying and listening to. But how can they do that when the kids are raising themselves? Mama may be working two jobs or the night shift trying to keep a roof over her family's head, and to ease her guilt, she buys her kid the latest MP3 player or cell phone and has no idea what music they're downloading. Daddy either isn't in the picture or takes a "hands-off" attitude; anyway, in most cases, neither of them would probably bother to say or do anything about it.

At one time, you couldn't even see a married couple sleeping in the same bed on a TV show, now not only are they sleeping, but they're also screwing. The movies are no exception...what once was considered R-rated when I was growing up is now commonly depicted in PG-13 movies. The movie producers put the ratings on their movies and the movie theaters put up their warning signs about patrons under 17 having to be accompanied by an adult to see an R rated flick, but my question is, why would an adult with any sense of decency about them take their minor child to what is supposed to be an adult movie?

When a country turns its back on what was once the reason

for its rise to power, it is bound to fall. Religion played a huge role in America's early moral development. Now it is treated like a pariah, except of course for those hypocritical, evangelical hustlers who are becoming rich by its misuse.

It's ok to display "In G_D We Trust" on coinage, but you better not say his name or make any reference to him when praying at a public event. Even though school children recite the words "One nation, under G_D" every morning in the classroom, they can't use school space to have bible study during lunch if they want, or have an afterschool club that studies the biblical material of any type; they call it violating constitutional separation of church and state.

Cities all over the US have lawsuits to keep the Ten Commandments or a nativity scene from being displayed in public buildings or on public grounds, yet go into the courtroom where the case is being heard and you may see "In G_D We Trust" embedded on the walls. What hypocrisy! What all these political officials forget is that they exist because G_D allows them to exist. He is "the Most High that rules in the kingdom of men, gives it to whomever He will, and sets over it the *lowest* of men" (Daniel 4:17).

History has taught the lesson well that the moral character of a nation is an important component of its existence. The moral law of G_D applies to nations as well as to individuals. G_D's word says "Do not be deceived; G_D is not mocked; for whatever a man sows, that he will also reap" (Galatians 6:7). This means that individuals and nations that sow immorality, violence and oppression will not long endure.

America is immoral, violent and oppressive. Its decline is inevitable and I am not alone in this belief. Former US Education Secretary William Bennett was well aware of America's decay when he wrote "If lying, manipulation, sloth, lack of discipline, and personal irresponsibility become commonplace, the national economy grinds down…Just as there are enormous financial benefits to moral health, there are enormous financial costs to moral collapse."[1]

While he was researching decadence in modern society, Jim Nelson Black listed such signs of decay as "luxury, skepticism, weariness, superstition... a preoccupation with self... promotion of the wrong people, the urge to overspend, and a rise of 'liberal opinion'—that is, the popularization of attitudes and policies controlled by sentiment rather than sound moral judgment."[2]

Black's words resound with truthfulness when you look at what is important to Americans today. Celebrities, be they athlete, actor, or entertainer, are promoted as "role models" and people to be imitated and adored. The economy is collapsing around the huge debts racked up by the government and individuals, neither of whom is content to live within their means. The acceptance of young men (and grown men who should know better) walking around with their pants hanging off their ass is a "popularization of attitudes"; ask them why they do it and all they can say is "that's how I wear them" or "it's the style" or even "what you want me to do, wear them like Urkel?" Even when you tell them that the practice originated in the prisons as a way for one man to signify to another that he is available for sex, they are not moved to pull them up...

Previously, I stated that the fall of America most closely resembles that of the Roman Empire. Let me elaborate on that... the Roman Empire began as a moral and disciplined nation, as did colonial America. The family unit was important and the rock that the Roman society was built upon. As it progressed into the second century, the societal fabric began to fray and family life began to erode as parents lost control of their offspring, indulging them to the point of creating a generation of lazy and undisciplined citizens. The people became apathetic and immune to the corruption of their government officials, more concerned with the debauchery of the theater, which was their primary means of entertainment and evidence of their declining morality.[3] Sounds familiar, doesn't it?

American families today are experiencing disintegration reminiscent of the Romans. Many parents are afraid of their own so called children, another sign of our declining morality. You hear parents saying things like 'I'm gonna beat the hell out of you!' and 'what in the hell is wrong with you?' or 'who in the hell do you think you are?' What is the problem here? The Holy Qur'an among others says that we all have guardian angels and if you believe that then you will also understand that angels do not dwell in unclean places... there are two places that angels do not go; they do not go into the bathroom nor do they go behind the closed doors of your bedroom. However there is still supposed to be order maintained in that privacy, because there must be order when you approach G_D.

Now for understanding and clarification, I ask, do you say a blessing before you begin to eat? If so, you are following order, because wherever there are two or more present there is always a third party present, that third party being Satan; therefore you un-invite him. When you go behind closed doors with your partner you should always ask G_D to go with you; I know you are prob-ably thinking how controversial is that? But if you keep asking your child the same questions over and over, "what in the hell is wrong with you?", "who in the hell do you think you are?", "what in the devil is your problem?" or saying "I'm gonna beat the hell out of you"... you must remember that you too were a child and perhaps you should consider asking your parents the same burning ques-tions you asked yourself. Maybe it is time to consider whether or not they uninvited the devil (that third party) when you were being conceived. If you figure that out then you can figure out the rest of your child's problems and yours too; then and only then can we begin to understand our behaviors from a spiritual as well as a carnal standpoint.

It is said in the book of Genesis... "There will come a time when children will be easy to be led in the wrong direction and hard to be led in the right direction" and this is prophetic truth, because it is happening today. Those children being led in the wrong direction are primarily young black males. Ask a Black boy in urban schools between the ages of 5 and 12 what they want to be when they grow up, and they will invariably tell you a professional basketball or football player, or a rapper (of course there are exceptions!). The media puts forth images that glamorize the lifestyle of having mad money and luxury cars, holding these out as the only role models or careers to which a black male can aspire. Now, there's nothing wrong with having a dream to play in the NBA or NFL or rap before a concert hall full of your peers, but when that is all that is placed before a young man without helping him to understand that there is no college degree in football or basketball, then a disservice is being done.

Those same boys, by the time they reach 16 years of age have become so disillusioned with their prospects, they resort to selling drugs on the street or stealing cars, robbing stores, committing burglaries, etc., to make a few dollars. When you look at the statistics of black males being removed from the general school population for having drugs or selling drugs at school, you will see that some have started as early as 6th grade! Trying to turn these boys around is a near impossible feat.

Statistics bear out the truth that the vast majority of black males in prison were raised in single parent, female-headed households. Once released on probation, lacking education or job skills, many may end up on the streets dealing drugs or addicted to drugs, as their prospects of finding sustainable employment are dim.

Once we the people get to know ourselves as G_D created us, we become impervious to all that has kept us frail, weak and easily influenced to go down the wrong path rather than travel the right road.

A large portion of the blame for the moral decline of the American empire rests with those we elect to represent us, similar to the Roman Empire. The politicians love to end their speeches with "G_D Bless America!" even after they've committed atrocities against G_D's creations. G_D can't bless what he abhors; therefore He cannot bless a nation that practices immorality, deceit, violence and oppression. Leaders of this nation have engaged in immoral and even criminal activities under the guise of "national security" for years. Like the Romans, the American people turn a blind eye to the corrupt actions of our government leaders and dismiss stories of the government's involvement in events like the assassinations of John F. Kennedy (America is the only industrialized superpower that has assassinated its own leader, one who was chosen through the democratic process), Robert Kennedy, Malcolm X, Martin Luther King, Jr., 9/11, and the introduction of cocaine into the urban neighborhoods of LA during the 80s, as wild conspiracy theories, despite the voluminous evidence supporting the allegations.

Take for instance, the George HW Bush (#41)-CIA-Bill Clinton drug smuggling connection to a little airport in Mena, Arkansas during Clinton's years as governor of that state. While Bill Clinton was governor of Arkansas, he was involved in protecting CIA-sponsored shipments of arms to the Nicaraguan Contra rebels in return for cocaine from Colombia, through the Mena, Arkansas airport. Mena became Clinton's ticket to the Whitehouse. How? …Clinton had the goods on Bush and Bush had the goods on Clinton; with their shared secret, they knew one wouldn't rat out the other. Why do you think Bill Clinton and George HW Bush are such good buddies these days? It's because Bush can claim that Clinton allowed the Mena Connection, the gateway for Colombian drugs to enter the U.S. via the airport in Mena and provided the means to launder the money earned from the cocaine sales. Clinton can claim that Bush authorized and supervised the CIA-run operation. Clinton ignored the activities of the CIA at Mena right up until he began his bid for the presidency, and even then he only paid lip service to investigating any of the allegations that were being made public.[4]

He could have used the Bush regime's war crimes in Central America and Iraq, the dealings with Saddam prior to his invasion of Kuwait, or the CIA drug business to bring the hammer down on George 41 when he ascended to the presidency, but doing so would have been like biting off his nose to spite his face.

For all the years during the Reagan/Bush presidencies that the "war on drugs" was being fought, it couldn't be won because they were fighting against themselves. It has been reported that while George Herbert Walker Bush was the director of the CIA, and on into his vice presidency under Ronald Reagan, the CIA conspired with the Colombian drug cartels and drug kingpin Barry Seal to smuggle cocaine into the United States. Some of the cocaine was sold to the Bloods and Cripps gangs in Los Angeles, beginning the devastation of the crack epidemic in Black neighborhoods. The money from the sale of the cocaine was used to finance the subversive activities of the CIA in South America. There is damning evidence about Bush's involvement and Clinton's knowledge of it in court documents, numerous blogs and newspaper archives like the Wall Street Journal, the Arkansas Times, and the San Jose Mercury News, not to mention video interviews (see *Clinton Coke Lines* on www.video.google.com) and books written by the people involved in the investigation of the activities at Mena as well as the smuggling operation itself.

This was not the first time the American government, via the CIA, brought drugs into the country. During the Indochina war in the late 60's and early 70's, the CIA operated a company called Air America that was used to smuggle heroine into the US. At the same time, tens of thousands of US soldiers stationed in Southeast Asia become addicted to heroine and returned home as junkies. For years, the CIA has facilitated the trafficking of drugs to pay for the weapons they supply to rebel organizations fighting against governments the US finds unfriendly towards or unsupportive of US policies, be it in Central America, Southeast Asia, Afghanistan or even Africa, often without the knowledge of other US agencies like the Drug Enforcement Agency, who may be engaged in their own secret activities. When their exploits come to light, the national media don't pursue the stories because the owners of the major papers and broadcast companies often have ties to the political party in power at the time and the powers-that-be squash the stories, or hide behind their favorite line "it's in the best interests of national security not to allow so-and-so to testify or be interviewed." How could G_D bless a nation with a terroristic government that drugs its own citizens for personal, financial and political gain?

How could G_D bless a nation that poisoned and conducted radiation experiments on its own citizens? From the 1940s through the 1970s, varying government agencies, specifically the Atomic Energy Commission and the Manhattan Project, exposed unsuspecting Americans to radiation. One experiment in particular, injected terminally ill patients with plutonium so the government could collect research data on the safety standards for weapons production. They conducted these and other experiments on the elderly, prison inmates, the mentally retarded, even children and pregnant women. Many others were deceived about the nature of the "treatments" they were receiving. From 1960 to 1971, the US military sponsored an experiment with the University of Cincinnati where 88 cancer patients between the ages of 9 and 94 were exposed to massive doses of radiation and data was collected on their physiological and psychological responses. The purpose: so the military could determine how much radiation a soldier could withstand before becoming disabled in the event of a nuclear detonation![5] These and other terroristic acts by the US military were brought to light in April of 1994 by Eileen Welsome, a journalist for the Albuquerque (NM) Tribune.

How could G_D bless a nation with a government that stood by while its own citizens were attacked by "public servants" with dogs, fire hoses and batons? Or that would plan the premeditative murder of thousands of its own people, as the Bush (43) administration did on September 11, 2001?

The 9/11 conspiracy has added to the shame and embarrassment we as a nation have endured before the world. The collapse of the Twin Towers was murder by proxy. How much did the Bush administration know and when did they know it? What did they do to prevent or thwart the needless murder of thousands of innocent citizens, or were they the masterminds behind it?

After reading numerous reports, documents and news stories, as well as viewing videos related to the incident, I have concluded as have so many others, that the Bush administration and those closest to it, came up with the scheme to create the 9/11 debacle as a pretense for war. They knew that if they could start wars in Afghanistan and Iraq, they stood to make massive amounts of money. For example, according to an article posted on 911truth. org, an unknown number of speculators used their first hand knowledge of the occurrence of 9/11 events to profit from insider trading, including "put options" to short-sell American and United Airlines stock.[6] There are documents, including memos and emails, from within the Bush Administration, that detail conversations about removing Saddam Hussein as much as 8 months *before* the 9/11 event. Former Treasury Secretary Paul O'Neill revealed first hand information about these discussions in an interview with Lesley Stahl of *60 Minutes* in January of 2004 and in the book *The Price of Loyalty* by Ron Suskind.[7]

There is a powerful, internet-based documentary-style movie called "Zeitgeist: The Movie" that is a scathing indictment of the collusion that took place between George W. Bush, Dick Cheney and their private moneymen, to create an incident that would provide a pretense to go to war. There is obviously truth behind the details because every time the producer of the 5-part series posts his movie on YouTube, the moderators (or as I prefer to call them, the Bush Censurers) of YouTube take it down off the site! If you want to see the entire, two hour documentary, you need to go to Google Video.

Congresswoman Cynthia McKinney launched an inquiry about this conspiracy by the Bush administration and their role in the senseless murders of thousands of innocent people. To discredit her, Bush supporters portrayed Congresswoman Cynthia McKinney as a fool or some crazy who had suddenly lost her mind; but it wasn't because of the accusation but rather due to the audacity of the Bush administration and their continued disregard for the constitution and the lack of respect for American lives that were lost because this administration considered them expendable on behalf of self interest.

There are some damning facts about what George Bush and Dick Cheney knew, dating back to George Bush 41 and Bill Clinton (yes, Wild Bill), about the premeditated attacks that were engineered with American involvement at the highest levels.

Consider this from the Public Education Center (PEC):

1. The congressional 9/11 committee, chaired by Senator Bob Graham and Congressman Porter Gross, ignored an allegation that just prior to September 11th, Mahmud Ahmed, the chief of the Pakistani intelligence agency, ISI, wired $100,000 to Mohamed Atta, identified as the mastermind behind the hi-jacking of the airliners. On the morning of 9/11, Sen. Graham and Rep. Gross held a meeting on Capitol Hill with none other than *Mahmud Ahmed!*

2. The Bush Administration's assertion that the 9/11 attacks were a surprise can be disputed by the existence of court records from the 1997 trial of Ramiz Yousef, a Pakistani terrorist described as the mastermind behind the 1993 WTC bombings.

   Those documents indicate that the CIA and FBI knew as far back as 1995 that plans existed to crash planes into selected US targets. The plot was discovered by Philippine authorities in January of 1995 when they seized a computer from an apartment used by Ramiz,

Ahmed Murad and one other man, all of whom were associated with Bin-Laden's al-Qaeda network. It detailed intentions to simultaneously explode 11 US airliners over the Pacific enroute from various Asian cities. There was also an alternative plan to hijack several planes and fly them into buildings that included the CIA headquarters, the World Trade Center, the White House and even the Sears Tower in Chicago. It was code named Project Bojinka.

While being extradited from Pakistan in February of 1995, Yousef boasted of the plot to Secret Service agent Brian Parr and FBI agent Charles Stern, both of whom later testified to that fact in court. Was it a coincidence that the date of Yousef's conviction for his role in this plot was 9/11/96?

3. After the exposure of Project Bojinka, the FBI began gathering evidence that international terrorists were training how to fly jumbo jets at American flight schools.[8]

Granted, there are many who will dismiss this as perpetuating the conspiracy theory, but the question that begs to be asked is, if the truth were really meant to be determined, why wasn't the 9/11 Commission granted subpoena power? Wasn't it imperative to get to the bottom of what happened so someone could be charged with a crime? After all, it was so important to find out what Slick Willy was doing with his wonka that Kenneth Starr was given subpoena power. Which truth has more value?

Like I said before, until America atones for the terrorism it has perpetrated on people here and abroad, it cannot heal the sickness within. Unless there is individual and *national* repentance, America will continue its decline into a moral abyss and eventual demise as an empire, one we'll only read about in a history book or see artifacts of in a museum some day.

America began its empire building on the backs of the Native Americans with the stealing of their land, the Africans brought here forcibly and inhumanely to be enslaved, as well as "immigrants" like the Chinese and the Irish. I use immigrants loosely because the capitalists that run this country and control its economy seem to have forgotten that by definition, they too are immigrants, by way of their ancestors. When the English explorers came to the New World, it was economic gain and greed that drove them. Tales of riches to be found and "free" land danced like sugar plums in their heads.

Like the medieval fiefdoms, the European immigrant, aka "American" white male, was intent on developing and maintaining a way of life that required the labor of serfs, otherwise known as the subservient or subordinate individual who "paid" for their passage to this new land of opportunity by indenturing themselves to the wealthy "nobles." In order to keep their notion of "superiority", the indentured servant and later, the African slave, was relegated to the lowest rungs of society by their wealthy white male "owners" and kept in the poorest conditions, being forced to live in substandard or squalid housing, the beginnings of the modern day underclass…there is no such thing as a classless society, which many (read: the elite) assert we live in.

Then, as now, an underclass consisting of low-wage (or no wage) workers was necessary for the ruling class to maintain and increase their wealth and power. According to Freidrich Engels, "only when he himself is wholly released from labour does the employer of labour become a true capitalist." In fact, capitalism cannot exist without an underclass of underemployed and unemployed workers. Karl Marx was the first to describe this manipulation by corporate owners. By forcing people to compete for jobs, they are able to keep wages low, thus making more money for themselves and their stockholders.

The Congress of these United States has been a co-conspirator by refusing to increase the minimum wage to a livable wage, effectively guaranteeing the continuation of the underclass. Those unfortunate individuals unable to secure a job year after year eventually quit trying, thereby establishing a permanent underclass and becoming what John Maynard Keynes described as "the involuntary unemployed". As a matter of fact, a recent work experience summary released by the US Bureau of Labor Statistics reported that about 3.2 million individuals looked for a job but did not work at all in 2008, up from 2.1 million in 2007 and the number of persons who experienced some unemployment in 2008 increased by 6.1 million to 21.2 million.[9] The "American Dream" has become a nightmare for the millions who are disenfranchised.

In economic circles, the argument about the causes of unemployment and its impact on the economy is an age old one. According to Keynes' thinking, when businesses have a negative outlook on profits, they tend to reduce the amount of money they invest. This leads to a reduction in the demand for goods, which reduces the production of those goods, which in turn leads to a reduction in employment, thereby causing an increase in unemployment.

A vicious cycle then begins, as household incomes fall and people don't have the money to make the purchases they used to make. Before John Keynes, economists believed that this cycle would right itself naturally if the unemployed reduced their salary expectations (work for less money) and the government stayed out of the fray. Keynes did not believe this and put forth a theory that when the economy is in a slump and the nation is not at full employment, it becomes necessary for the government to intervene to bring things back into balance by either putting money into the economy or reducing taxes, which would theoretically put more money into the pockets of the workers.

In developing what became the capitalistic system, the white males who had the money and the land, also developed the laws by which they lived. Those laws frequently benefitted one small segment (white males) while discriminating against the majority, including white women. Anything that threatened the white male dominance was fought against with ferocity, including affording women the right to vote and abolishing slavery. Sociopolitical essayist Jason Miller wrote "...our founders created a nation which afforded freedom and equality almost exclusively to that of white males who possessed a measure of wealth" and "American capitalism is a pyramid scheme shaped and forged over time to ensure that a small minority of principally white males garner a majority of the wealth."[10] His statement is borne out by the following statistics as compiled by Edward Wolff, an economist at New York University and reported on the website *Who Rules America.net:*

"In terms of types of financial wealth, the top one percent of households has 38.3% of all privately held stock, 60.6% of financial securities, and 62.4% of business equity. The top 10% have 80% to 90% of stocks, bonds, trust funds, and business equity, and over 75% of non-home real estate. Since financial wealth is what counts as far as the control of income-producing assets, we can say that just 10% of the people own the United States of America."[11]

The American capitalistic pyramid scheme is located in the Middle East; we are sold the dream that if we buy a little piece of the pie, we can parlay it into great wealth but first we have to start at the Mediterranean or Baltic. If we play the game long enough we're led to believe we can trade up, but by and large, the white patriarchal, financial elite (the 10%) already has a strong hold on the premium choices like Park Place and the Boardwalk, while those of us less fortunate (the 90%) go directly to jail, do not pass Go or collect anything or are stuck in the Mediterranean or Baltic. Pardon the humor, but we must maintain the ability to laugh and joke while at the same time making a profound point.

I'm sure that if you've read this far that by now you may have established the opinion that this book is about bashing the white male and blaming him for the problems of people of color, here and abroad. As I said in the foreword I assure you this is not about black versus white. Unfortunately, the white man does bear the burden for much of the ills that this country faces because he has been the one controlling the purse strings and making the decisions as the powerbrokers. I have to bring the truth to the forefront because in order to make changes and move forward, in hopes of forestalling the decline of this great nation, one has to know the past in order to understand the present.

Criticism without suggestions for change is not constructive. Presenting problems without making recommendations for solutions is not constructive. The aim of this book is to bring about change through provoking thought.

Notes

1. William Bennett. *Death of Outrage: Bill Clinton and the Assault on American Ideals.* (New York: Simon and Schuster, Inc., 1998)

2. Jim Nelson Black. *When Nations Die: America on the Brink, Ten Warning Signs of a Culture in Crisis.* (Illinois: Tyndale House Publishers, 1995)

3. Jerome Carcopino. *Daily Life in Ancient Rome: The People and the City at the Height of the Empire.* Edited and annotated by Henry T. Roswell. Yale University Press, 1968

4. Paul DeRienzo. *Arkansas Governor Bill Clinton, President George (H.W.) Bush, CIA Drugs for Guns Connection.* N.C.O.I.C. Civil Intelligence Association, Defense Oversight Group (n.d.) http://www.ncoic.com/clinton.htm   Retrieved 1/26/2010

5. Judith Braffman-Miller. *When medicine went wrong: how Americans were used illegally as guinea pigs.* USA Today (Society for the Advancement of Education, March 1995. Posted on BNET http://findarticles.com//p/articles/mi_ m1272/is_n2598_v123/ai_16805720/?tag=content;col Retrieved 2/20/2010

6. 911truth.org. *Insider Trading,* cited from *Insider Trading Apparently Based on Foreknowledge of the 9/11 attacks* (London Times, 9/18/2001) http://www.911truth.org

7. CBS News: *Saddam's Ouster Planned in '01?* Posted 1/10/2004 on commondreams.org http://www.commondreams.org/headlines04/0110-03.htm

8. Public Education Center (PEC) Report. *Terrorist Plans to Use Planes as Weapons date to 1995: WTC Bomber Yousef confesses to US agents in 1995*. Public Education Center, Washington, DC http://www.publicedcenter.org/faaterrorist.htm

9. U.S. Bureau of Labor Statistics. *Work Experience Summary*. December 8, 2009 http://www.bls.gov/news.release/work.nr0.htm

10. Jason Miller. *American Capitalism and the Moral Poverty of Nations*. Posted 5/29/2006 http://www.worldphilosophy.cn/html/haiwaishuping/200909/20-561.html

11. G. William Domhoff. *Who Rules America: Wealth, Income and Power*. Retrieved from http://sociology.ucsc.edu/whorulesamerica/power/wealth.html

"It is natural and just for nations, peoples and individuals to demand respect for their rights and freedoms and to struggle to end oppression, racism, economic exploitation, military occupation, and various forms of colonialism and alien domination."

The Dalai Lama in his submission to the 1993 "United Nations World Conference on Human Rights"

CHAPTER 2

A Rogue Nation on the Decline

America is a rogue nation as much as I hate to say it, but it is true. I love this country but despise what it represents as well as its founding principles (lies, murder, rape, thievery and yes, slavery!!!). America will continue its downward spiral into a moral abyss until its empire has been completely lost if change does not come and come quickly. The first change that needs to take place is an apology to those that America enslaved and betrayed, has repeatedly refused to apologize to for building the American "kingdom" on their backs and that is in accordance with the Christian doctrine that is so widely and heavily entrenched into the very fiber that America prides itself on and wraps itself around.

The horror of slavery is akin to the horror of the Holocaust. Many of you readers won't like that I said that, but nevertheless, it's true. Think about it, Hitler and his Nazi followers believed themselves to be superior to not just the Jews, but the cripples and mentally deficient, the Jehovah's Witnesses, the gypsies; anyone not "blonde and blue-eyed Aryans". It was not necessary to treat them with any form of humanity or compassion, because they were considered less than human. Well, that was the same mentality of the white man when he enslaved the African and subjected an entire race of people to economic genocide. To understand the conditions that exist in Black America today, you have to revisit the ugly history of slavery, for there is where the white man began his campaign to build his empire on the backs of others.

Put yourself in the chains of the men, women and children who were ripped from their motherland and forced to endure the brutal and inhumane conditions aboard the slave ship as it made its journey to Europe, and later, America:

> "...the slaves were all enclosed under grated hatchways between decks. The space was so low that they sat between each other's legs and were stowed so close together that there was no possibility of their lying down or at all changing their position by night or day...the cells were three feet high...shut out from light or air...The space between decks was divided into two compartments 3 feet 3 inches high, one being 16 feet by 18 feet ...into which 226 women and girls were crammed, the second being 40 by 21 with 336 men and boys...Some were greatly emaciated and some, particularly the children, seemed dying... It was not surprising that they should have endured much sickness and loss of life in the ...17 days they had been out...they had thrown overboard no less than 55 who had died of dysentery and other complaints...I was informed by my friends....that this was one of the best (ships) they had seen...They had on one occasion taken a slave vessel... the slaves were...chained together...manacled together in twos and threes. Sometimes of the three attached to the same chain, one was dying and another was dead. Many destroyed one another in the hopes of (gaining) more room to breathe; men strangled those next to them, and women drove nails into each other's brains. Many unfortunate creatures on other occasions took the first opportunity of leaping overboard and getting rid, in this way, of an intolerable life."[1]

Now that you have that picture in your mind, picture this...

Imagine being chained in an 8 square foot hole in a rock with 29 others, a 5 kilogram metal ball permanently chained to your neck or foot, knowing that any attempt at escape means sure death as you drown in the deep waters of the Atlantic. You have just stepped through the "Door of No Return" on Goree Island. Imagine that for the next 300 years, your children and your children's children will be forced to endure these same wretched conditions, never to see their homeland or loved ones again.

Imagine your mother, your wife, your children and yourself, lying naked in your own urine and feces, breathing the stench of 400 others shackled like you, in the cramped bowels of the slave ship, week after week. You are sick from the constant rocking and rolling of the ship and choke on your vomit as you lay on your back. There are so many of you crammed like sardines in a can that you can't stand, you can't change positions, you can't move from one endless day to the next. You hear your mother, your wife, your children, moaning and crying out in pain from sickness and hunger, yet you can do nothing to comfort them. Imagine how you must feel as a man, knowing that your family is dying and you are helpless, powerless to save them.

Finally, the motion of the ship comes to an end and you think your journey has too. See the confusion on the faces of your family (if they survived) as they step out into the sunlight and gaze upon an unfamiliar land. Imagine the fear that your mother, your wife and your children feel as they watch you being sold and led away in chains in one direction, while they are led in another to begin a life of wretched oppression, discrimination and racism from which there is no end.

I bet you had a hard time putting yourself in the shoes of the African slave and by extension, Black Americans, especially if you're of the Caucasian persuasion. That's the problem with this country today and why G_D will not bless America. This is what Jeremiah Wright meant when he said "G_D Damn America".

Remember that a nation that practices oppression cannot prosper because G_D does not like ugly. The oppression that began with slavery continues to the present day. African Blacks, particularly Black males were a commodity and are treated as so today.

As one would know, a commodity is something to be bought, sold or traded for something else of value. That something of value is the perpetuation of the capitalistic economic system. As stated previously, America needs a permanent underclass and needs to keep adding to that underclass. This is accomplished by ensuring that a portion of the society is unemployable. A large portion of that unemployable group consists of black males, many of whom have left school without the skills necessary to be legitimate productive members of society. Unable to participate in the mainstream economy, they become engaged in the underground economy of illegal activities.

Here is where the commodity trading begins. Statistics show that more and more African-American families are headed by females and a large portion of these families live in poverty. Removal of the black male, a practice that began with slavery, and now accomplished through prison sentences or black-on-black murder, destroys the nucleus of the black family. According to the US Department of Justice report on Prison and Jail Inmates at Midyear 2006, more black men (836,800) were in custody in a state, federal or local jail, than their white counterparts (718,100). These statistics are the result of a lack of positive black role models. If the black male is removed or painted in a light other than positive, the young black male is left without the understanding of the nucleus or what it means to raise a family within the mainstream economic system.

The commodity trading is completed when the black male is released from prison and is unable to secure gainful employment or can only secure minimum wage employment, thereby joining the ranks of the unemployed and/or underemployed. The children of these men grow up without working fathers or the notion that working is an adult expectation.[2] A sense of hopelessness develops in them when they realize their access to opportunities afforded to others is limited. Having no role models in the community, they fail to develop a work ethic and eventually fall into the same trap of under education, underemployment, and participation in the underground economy, perpetuating the growth of the underclass. This perpetuates the breakdown of the black family, which results in the black female having to become the role model for the black male. I call this the AAFTA: African-American Fair Trade Agreement.

Now, if America intends to start the healing process from the atrocities that were committed against the Indians, and the Africans brought to America against their will (and continue to have to stay here because of the permanent uprooting and displacement of a people), this is the time to right the wrongs that were done; the wrongs that continue to have lingering effects.

Everything in America is determined by either race, class, good or bad, what you should do as opposed to what you shouldn't do, right or wrong, etc., but of course in America these concepts only apply when it comes to the subordination of people of color to whites. But, the pendulum is beginning to swing in the other direction. Once people of color were considered the minority but according to an August 2008 report by the U.S. Census Bureau, those groups currently categorized as racial minorities—blacks and Hispanics, East Asians and South Asians—will account for a majority of the U.S. population by the year 2042.

Why is this reality? Because in just one year alone, between July 1, 2006 and July 1, 2007, the Hispanic population grew by 3.3%, the Asian population grew by 2.9%, and the Black population grew by 1.9% while the white population only grew by 0.3%! The white population as a whole is older and when you look at the population in terms of those under the age of 18, **people of color already outnumber whites**. In 2007, almost 34 percent of the

Hispanic population was younger than 18, about 31 percent of the black population was younger than 18, about 27 percent of the Native American (Indian and Alaskan) population was younger than 18, and about 29 percent of the Native Hawaiian and Other Pacific Islander population was younger than 18, compared with only 21 percent of the white population being under 18! [3]

The modern day white male is in a struggle; he is a victim of his own circumstances.

In order for America to maintain its identification as a majority white nation, it has to have a renewable source of individuals to add to the pool. Geopolitically, the issue of race isn't just determined by the color of your skin but more so by the geographic location of one's country of origin. For example, when Middle Easterners migrate to America and become citizens, they and their American-born children are considered white. When Africans from the northern part of that country, like Morocco, migrate to America, geopolitically speaking, they are considered white, when in truth, they are African Americans in every sense of the word! As a matter of fact, if you took a scientific look at skin color, which is used to determine race in America, EVERYBODY is black! Studies of mitochondrial and chromosomal DNA indicate that modern humans are descended from dark-skinned humans who migrated out of southern Africa about 100,000 years ago.[4] As humans migrated to the northern climates, skin color gradually became lighter as an adaptation to the less intense sunlight. Today, because of continued migrations, many people no longer live in the environments for which their skin was adapted. Now, that's the official scientific version; my version is a little more controversial.

When you consider skin color, you have to consider the sciences of the anatomy and the germination process. In order to get a lighter color, one would have to start with a dark color first and this applies to all that G_D created from the beginning. When you take a dark germ and graft away from it, the result is a lighter or weaker germ. As far as the human element is concerned, this same principle applies. The black germ is the strongest of all as science says that dark traits are always dominant to light traits. Therefore, when you take a black germ and graft away from it (i.e. mix it with another race) you may get a brown germ; graft again and you may get a yellow germ; keep grafting away and eventually, you get a white germ. With each grafting, the resulting germ gets weaker until eventually you have something that is void of color and strength, being easily tempted, susceptible to sickness and disease, for it has been weakened to the point where it cannot fend for itself.

Evidence of my theory is supported by historical fact, for history is best qualified to reward research. During the latter part of the nineteenth century when the British began migrating to their imperial colony in Calcutta, India, they found the tropical climate to be taxing to their health. They had no immunity to the regional diseases and less than half of the English and Scottish immigrants who came to Calcutta in its first century survived to return back home. It became a badge of honor to survive the hot summer months so much so that every November, when the cool season began, they would meet to congratulate one another on having survived another year![5]

Truth be told and this is a fact: if you put a black man and a white woman in a relationship and out of that coming together a child emerges, he/she is black. If you put a black woman and a white man in a relationship and a child emerges, he/she is black. Why Black and not bi-racial you say? The historian Matthew Frye Jacobson asked, "Why is it that in the United States, a white woman can have black children but a black woman cannot have white children?" Because history determines the race of those children: remember the "one drop" rule? If you had one octoroon or 1/8th of black blood in you then you were a nigger; well, that same principle applies today because of historical truth. This race of babies being born of these circumstances may be considered biracial children but according to America's own admissions they are niggers!

What of the so-called multi-racial child, you know, like Tiger Woods, who is one quarter Chinese, one quarter Thai, one quarter African American, one eighth American Indian and one eighth Dutch (his great grandfather on his mother's side was a Dutchman). His father was of mixed African American, Chinese and Native American ancestry and his mother is of mixed Thai, Chinese and Dutch ancestry, but when Americans see Tiger, they see a black man!

Now how do you think Tiger will identify his race on the 2010 census? What about his children, since they are born to a "black" man and a "white" woman? Are they black? According to America's one drop rule, he AND his children are BLACK. However, he will have a host of races to select from when he completes the 2010 census. Where once there were only 4 categories from which to select your race, Black, White, Asian or Pacific Islander, and Native American or Alaska native; there are now 16 separate racial categories from which to select, and not just Tiger, but any one of us, can choose more than one category. For 2010, the Asian category has been separated into Chinese, Filipino, Japanese, Korean, Vietnamese or Other Asian and the Pacific Islander category has been divided so that Native Hawaiians can identify themselves separately from other Pacific Islanders, each of whom also have *their* own separate category, ostensibly to reflect the great diversity of people living in these United States of America!
6

The reason I am telling you this is so there is no more confusion. When we discuss race in America, we speak of races from an historical and religious perspective. If we speak about religion, we must understand and know history. You cannot qualify one without the other. In fact everything that you do is based on history. Even if it comes down to choosing the color you want to paint your house or the food that you eat, it's all based on history. It is history that influences your decisions; through history you determine your likes and dislikes. By ignoring or denying history, be we individuals or a nation, we deny our selves.

So, when we look at the issues in their rightful perspective America, you must be truthful if you really want to make a change for the better. It has always been said that "if you really want forgiveness then you have to be sincere in your heart and the only way to get into heaven is to not yield to hypocrisy"; spiritually or biblically speaking the only one that cannot go to heaven is the hypocrite! America what are you going to do now that you have the chance to right the wrong that was done to the Africans and other people of the world that you misused and abused? You have the chance to at least take a step in the direction of atonement by doing something good for the Iraqi people, and all the other refugees created by the colonial invasions of the American government in its attempt to usurp control of energy resources in their scheme to achieve global dominance, particularly on the continent of Africa.

When you have power, you have to be willing to be fair and equitable in the universal distribution of economic development and political clout, as well as allowing the people their constitutional right to speak. ... Patrick Henry said "give me liberty or give me death" and America stood by him and by goodness they fought a bloody war and it was okay, but when Malcolm X said " by any means necessary" America accosted him, put a contract on him marked for death. When young Emmett Till whistled at the white woman, he died for it, yet you don't hear about a white boy being killed for even raping a black woman.

Blacks in America don't have equality but *equality by constituted authority* which is, by the way, why whites in this country and throughout the world will not respect Black Americans, because they do not respect constituted authority. The white man has always had to be forced (legislated) to do what's right because he has never had any intention of sharing this country with his former slaves; it's just not inherent in his heart or soul. As far as he was (and still is) concerned, the Black man was (and is) not a citizen of this country and the protections of the Constitution didn't (and still don't) apply to him; in fact, the Dred Scott case of 1857 formerly established that Blacks were not citizens of this country. In his opinion for the court, the Chief Justice of the Supreme Court, Roger Taney, openly stated that even freed Blacks were not citizens, and never could be and since they weren't citizens they didn't have the right to sue. He wrote "The African race in the United States, even when free, are everywhere a degraded class, and exercise no political influence. The privileges they are allowed to enjoy are accorded to them as a matter of kindness and benevolence rather than of right...They're not looked upon as citizens by the contracting parties who formed the constitution. They were evidently not supposed to be included by the term 'citizens'." [7] It took a constitutional amendment (the 14th) nine years later to extend the status of citizenship to former slaves, and the 15th amendment a year after that to protect the former slaves' constitutional right to vote; not that it stopped the racism, discrimination and hatred perpetrated toward Blacks then nor now.

Most people, black and white alike, believe that the Emancipation Proclamation freed the slaves but it only freed those that lived in the states that had ceded from the Union and continued to fight against the Union. Issued three years into the Civil War, it didn't apply to the slave states of Delaware, Maryland, Kentucky and Missouri because they agreed to supply troops for Lincoln's armies (Delaware had actually already abolished slavery before the Proclamation was issued). It also didn't apply to the ceded (confederate) states that were already under the control of the Union army. Lincoln didn't issue the Proclamation because he cared so much about the slaves, because in his own words he believed blacks were inferior to whites. As a matter of fact, when he was campaigning for the Senate in 1858, he gave a speech refuting his support for equal treatment of blacks. In his own words: "I will say, then, that I am not, nor ever have been, in favor of bring-ing about in any way the social and political equality of the white and black races; that I am not, nor ever have been, in favor of making voters or jurors of Negros, nor of qualifying them to hold office, nor to intermarry with white people…And inasmuch as they cannot so live, while they do remain together, there must be the position of superior and inferior, and I as much as any other man am in favor of having the superior position assigned to the white race." [8]

As I said, his signing of the Emancipation Proclamation was not from the goodness of his heart, but rather as a war strategy to weaken the southern states and gain more soldiers since the Proclamation allowed Black men to join the Union army, even runaway slaves. What most people don't know and I don't recall ever seeing written in the history books used in schools, was that the freedom promised by the Proclamation was only valid if the north won the war! How fortunate for the black man that the north won (LOL!).

Notes

1. "Aboard a Slave Ship, 1829." Eyewitness to History. http://
    www.eyewitnesstohistorycom

2. David Whitman. *When Work Disappears: The World of the
    Urban Poor.* Washington Monthly, 11/1996.

3. U.S. Census Bureau News. *U.S. Hispanic Population Surpasses
    45 Million; Now 15% of Total.* Released May 1, 2008 http://
    www.census.gov/pressrelease/www/releases/archives/
    population/011910.htm

4. Patricia Schneider. *Case Teaching Notes for "The Case of
    Desiree's Baby: The Genetics and Evolution of Skin Color."*
    Queensborough Community College, Bayside, NY from the
    case studies of The National Center for Case Study in Teaching
    Science, 2003 http://www.sciencecases.org/skin_color/skin_
    color_notes.asp

5. Rhoads Murphey. *A Closer Look: Calcutta, Colonial Capital.*
    A History of Asia pg 302 (New Jersey: Pearson Education, Inc.
    2009)

6. Population Research Bureau (PRB). *The 2010 Census
    Questionnaire: 7 Questions for Everyone.* http://www.prb.
    orb/Articles/2009/questionnaire.aspx

7. Steve Mount. *Events Affecting the Constitution: Scott vs. Sandford
    (60 U.S. 393), 1857"* US Constitution.net Posted January 24, 2010
    http://www.usconstitution.net/events.html Retrieved 2/4/2010

8. Jim Hunt. *They Said What? Astonishing Quotes on
    American Democracy, Power and Dissent* pg 91 (California:
    PoliPointPress, Inc. 2009)

CHAPTER 3

The Hypocritical, Evangelical Hustlers

Earlier, I spoke of how the leaders of this country claim that their actions are blessed by "G_D", although they don't name the G_D of which they speak. We also have these so-called men of G_D, like Joel Osteen, who say the same thing. Forty years ago when his father started his ministry, there was starvation, hunger, sickness and disease in this nation and abroad. The younger Osteen, who has taken over those forty years of work his father left behind, claims that's a problem that cannot be fixed by him, yet he claims to serve a powerful G_D. If he and all the other hypocritical, evangelical hustlers like him, believe their "G_D" is so powerful, then why don't they call on their "G-D" to help them eradicate the evils of this world instead of just asking for "abundance" and financial gain?

I challenge all Christians, Jews, Gentiles, Muslims, Mormons and anyone who has the simple belief that G_D wants them to have abundance, to pray for the people in Somalia, Darfur, Rwanda, Botswana, Haiti and every other underdeveloped country where people are suffering, to have abundance and the pursuit of happiness; to have access to the internet, to have the freedom to live where they choose, to not go to bed hungry, to have good health and a legacy of security to pass on to their offspring. I challenge them all to fully share the abundance they have received from their "G_D" with those less fortunate than themselves, both here and abroad, in real ways and not just token donations or missionary visits that have more advantage to them than to the ones they are proclaiming to help.

We spend billions of dollars, year in and year out, on the space program, yet children and women in underdeveloped countries continue to go hungry, have no medical care for the most common ailments, have no sanitary drinking water, or nowhere to sleep; all the comforts most Americans take for granted. America may have money in the bank, but as a nation, it is morally bankrupt.

Joel Osteen has one of the largest and fastest growing ministries in the world; what work of G_D has he done with the wealth that he has amassed from portraying himself as a man of G_D? What about Jimmy Swaggert, James Robison, Oral Roberts and son, or Jim and the late Tammy Faye Bakker, not to mention the tens of thousands of not so famous preachers and pastors or even the Popes, all trying to get their hands in the pot!!! Last but not the least, Billy Graham, who's been around for nearly a hundred years; all the while, apartheid flourished alive and well. How many of the suffering children in the world have their ministries adopted? The world is full of death and destruction along with mayhem, horror, terror and human suffering, leaving the weak to be consumed by the strong...what animalistic behavior! We are supposed to be different from the animal creatures but are we?

I have a special bone to pick with the black men of G_D such as Fredrick Price, T.D. Jakes, and Kreflo Dollar who are failing to live up to their responsibilities, too. They are too concerned with their own images and do nothing to restore what slavery and systemic racism took away, the nucleus of the black family, the black man. When one enters into what co-author Bridget (Foster) McCoy calls "DeMamaNations" (since the vast majority of black church memberships consist of women) the focus is on the small group that may be members of their congregations, but there is no outreach of substance to those that are lost, specifically young black males who are or will become black fathers. What purpose does the preacher serve where black males and young black females are concerned? What are they doing to "lead them in the right direction"?

In discussions with close friends, we agree that the black male as a group has lost its identity. This is by design and began with slavery. The removal of the head of the family, the black man, was employed to gain control over the mental, physical and social development of blacks as a race. Carter G. Woodson wrote in 1933 that "when you control a man's thinking you do not have to worry about his actions because where you can control a man's mind you do not have to worry about what he is thinking and where you can control a man's thoughts you do not have to wonder about where he will go and if you send a man to the back door long enough he will always go to the back door even if there is no back door, he will make a back door and enter and he will do that as long as you can keep control of his mind."[1]

This is the very thing that destroys the black family in America: eliminating the nucleus, which happens to be the black father. The black mother is left to raise her black son without the guidance and modeling that should have been provided by the black man.

Seeing his mother provide the money, the food, etc. leaves the black male without an example of what a man is supposed to do. He grows up thinking that he doesn't have to provide for the household, the woman will; after all, his mother did...so as he comes into his manhood, he seeks the model with which he grew up. Once he begins producing offspring, he sees no need to have a role in the raising of that child, that is something that the female should be quite capable of doing...remember, that is the model with which he grew up.

As a result, he has nothing to pass on to his seed in terms of what the role and responsibility of a man is supposed to be, and this non-model is perpetuated over and over again, down through generations. It has the same impact on the female because the black daughter has no male model either. She learns how to take on the role of provider, protector and nurturer, contrary to what G_D intended. She too, has nothing to pass on to her offspring.

The black female is now twice-removed from the role that G_D intended...she is taken from motherhood to brotherhood, trying to do what she has had no training for or male to imitate, since she too, was raised without a black man. This is why the black woman is the backbone of not just the black race, but of this country. She didn't just raise her own children...she raised and nurtured the children of her white master as well.

This is why I hold the black preacher in such disdain. They should be teaching the black boy how to be a man and a provider, as G_D intended him to be. As followers and imitators of Jesus Christ, this is supposed to be their primary role, teaching others what G_D expects of them.

The black church, as a group, collects millions of dollars that could be used to uplift the community they are supposed to serve, but where are the schools, the businesses, the programs, etc. in the neighborhoods of their congregations? You don't have to pay to pray, and by the grace of G_D we are all saved, so when the church has reached its goals of membership, or the building fund, why not set up endowments to ensure independence in the black community? Economic independence is what the black community is in dire need of... to be providers and vendors and not just consumers. The black church should be taking the lead in these endeavors. They should take the lead in creating jobs in the community by building grocery stores, hospitals, drug stores, schools, etc. They could make the black community self-sustaining, so it can provide for itself what white America never will, economic parity.

The black preacher offers false hopes to the people he leads. He holds out the hope of blessings from G_D and ascension to heaven in exchange for the paying of tithes. They are misleading their congregations to think that if they use their rent or light bill money to tithe, they will be blessed by G_D when in fact all they will be is out the door or in the dark. The preachers keep their members literally in the dark because there is so much more that G_D expects from men who supposedly come in his name than just giving money to support a building and another man's standard of living.

Do the math... There is a terrible imbalance between the amount of money collected by Black churches of all denominations and the numbers of Blacks who benefit from the money collected. For as many years as Black churches have been in existence and collecting money from congregants, there should be many businesses, schools, hospitals, and drugstores, to name a few, built in black neighborhoods, creating self-sustained cities within cities.

G_D put us here to be of use to one another and to love one another, yet there are still women, babies, and children and whole nuclear families that have died leaving behind hundreds of thousands of orphans to fend for themselves; young girls having to take care of their younger siblings with no alternative but the sale of their young, innocent bodies for sex, many ending up on drugs, raped, and yes enslaved or murdered.

Kind of makes you wonder what G_D these men serve... most certainly not the G_D of creation of mankind and the world! I am curious why these so-called powerful men of G_D have done nothing with the millions they have amassed, except build a bigger church and buy a bigger car; while supposedly serving a most powerful G_D, and having influence all over the world...none of you powerful so-called men of G_D, used that influence along with your loudly proclaimed faith that G_D wants the same for those who are without, as he does for those who have, to eliminate the atrocities faced by so many people. Perhaps we need only refer to you as G_Dfathers or my personal favorite, hypocritical, evangelical hustlers, because, when you profess G_D as being your lord and the creator of all things, the infallible, the cherisher, and the sustainer of all things, those past and present, why then, won't you all stop talking about the unsearchable riches and abundance of life and share a fraction of it with those in need? Why don't you do like Bill Gates has done to make a true and lasting impact on the lives of others? Challenge each other like he challenged his billionaire counterparts to put up or shut up!

And you, America, you're contributing to the decline of this empire by supporting the lifestyles of these hustlers when you attend their mega churches and pay into their collection plates. Since when did G_D need your lowly, worthless "dollar" to do his work? They've got you fooled and the revolution demands that you take off your blinders and see them for the hustlers they are!

Notes

1. Carter G. Woodson. *The Mis-Education of the Negro.* Associated Publishers, 1933 Reprinted by Africa World Press, Inc. Trenton, NJ 1990

CHAPTER 4

Christianity Will Not Save A Nation In Decline

The leadership spout that America operates under the "Christian" method of thought, and lead us all down their path. In reality, they are using this jargon to convince the people they are good when it is evil that they are perpetuating in the name of Christianity. This is not a new tactic.

In the war on the Holy Land, St Peter's successors marched with the inscription "Deus Vult" ("G_D Wills It") and the Nazi's wore belt buckles with "Gott Mit Uns" (G_D With Us) decorating their uniforms. During Hitler's reign, the traditional crest was replaced by the Nazi swastika and eagle, however, the religious inscription "Gott Mit Uns", remained unaltered.

In his book *Forgotten Voices of the Great War*, Max Arthur wrote that part of the reason the Nazi government retained this motto was an attempt on the part of Hitler to retain the support of Christians, who comprised the overwhelming majority of German citizens.

One would think we would learn from the tragedies of the past. Murder and deception are not the "Christian" thing to do, nor is building the hopes and dreams of people, just to knock them down socially and economically when they become too powerful or too independent. I speak not only of this practice in other countries, but here in our own country. The Bush administration

(G.W. Bush) took on the guise of Christian Leadership and used it as sheep's clothing in hopes the people would follow, and they did, not once, but *twice!*

Leadership should be determined by how one takes a position to influence others to follow, recognizing the fact that a true leader understands that whatever happens to the leader is generally what will happen to the followers; therefore in order for America to hold on to its self-proclaimed lead it must be honest, stop lying, stop the murdering, stop the rape and thievery, and atone for what it has done to its own citizens as well as through proxy, to people of other nations. For anyone that says they love this country, in order to support that statement there has to be some truth to it; even though we no longer live under the Ten Commandments, we are still governed by the law of love, so when you say you love me, you do not steal from, kill, or destroy me.

Leadership is all about the consideration and respect that one demonstrates in their ability to lead…this is why it is so important for America to be under a good influence; that is a good contributing factor for having credibility… by showing honor even among your enemy. We have a duty to each other, ourselves and the world abroad, and that is to be true. There is no reality in America; it is all emblematic, which is why America is not capable of solving real problems.

Speaking of reality, let's start with the incipient stages of the development of this country, specifically the naming of America, which by the way should be called the United States of Cabot, because that is who is credited with the discovery of the land mass, John Cabot, not Christopher Columbus (the dumbass didn't even know where he was; he thought he was in Asia) or Amerigo Vespucci, which by the way is what the historians say. Vespucci is believed to have stolen the maps that John Cabot made of the New World after his voyage in 1497 and had his name attached to them. If this is so, it would explain why America is the way it is…for when a country is named after a liar and a thief, it is bound to take on the characteristics of which it was named after! The fact of the matter is, no one really knows who discovered this land mass called America, which reasserts my point that there is no reality in America.

We can never have a serious discussion about race and racism until whites in America recognize and give credit for all the good that blacks and other nonwhites have done for America; including being the chief executive officer (president)… yes that is right, America has already had a black president, so Barack Obama is not the first.[1] But there is never any realism in American politics or American history when dealing with real problems here as well as in the world. America will never address a real issue with more than superficiality simply because America only deals with sensationalism and does it very well because of the history for which it stands.

In keeping with its history of race, racism and racial politics, America chooses to ignore the role that enslaved as well as free blacks and other people of color, have played in the development of this country. White America has had a habit of rewriting and revising history through omission of facts that present them in an unflattering light. Until they can own up to their own misdeeds and mistreatment of the human lives that were used to build their empire, there will continue to be superficial solutions to the real problems this country faces.

Then and only then can America have real discussions about solving real problems such as: righting the wrongs of slavery, the truth about those individuals that are celebrated as founders of this great land known as America, uncovering the secrets about the United States and how it came to be, not to mention, the biggest secret of all which is how America came about its name. There is just so much work to be done not just among black people or white people but as a nation if there is ever to be a true discussion about race, religion, racism, history, or real forgiveness and atonement for what this government perpetrated and perpetuated.

Continue with the reality of the murders that took place in America beginning with the Native American Indians, on through the early- to- late 1600s which marked the beginning of the slave trade, to the present; America has never stopped…we have a war being fought right now that was started from lies being told, and as a result, over 4000 American troops and an undisclosed number (somewhere in the hundreds of thousands) of Iraqi citizens (and I haven't even counted the loss of life in Afghanistan!) have been "murdered"; yes I say *murdered* because, when you get a group of people together and say we are going to go over to somebody's house and kill them because somebody told a lie on them and you kill them for that reason it is called murder, no matter what you call yourself (i.e. army, navy, marines etc.). Murder is murder, especially when it is based on deceit or when you kill someone because of the color of their skin, their religious belief, or sexual orientation, or *natural resources!*

The reality is that America has had over 200 years of organized white leadership, under which no efforts have been made to right the wrongs, perhaps with the exception of land grants to certain Indian tribes, and the passage of the Civil Liberties Act of 1988 that paid reparations of $20,000 apiece to Japanese American citizens imprisoned during World War II. Yet, it was the black man who suffered over 400 years of discontent, including legal murder under the guise of Jim Crow laws, supported by the highest echelons of the American government, including and most especially the great Supreme Court, and nothing has been offered in the way of compensation, with the exception of individual state legislatures which have offered up token apologies in the form of proclamations, from which no descendant of any slave has benefited. If you can't take care of your own at home; if there is no respect for those murdered on your own grounds, how then can America expect to receive respect after committing legal murder in the form of the wars in Iraq and Afghanistan? And they (Washington bureaucrats) know who is next. *"When the tyrant has*

disposed of foreign enemies by conquest...and there is nothing to fear from them, then he is always stirring up some war"--------
Plato, ancient Greek philosopher

The reality is that America has a deep history of racism, a history that many in white America refuse to acknowledge or try to downplay by saying " I can't be held responsible for what people did before I was born" or "My family didn't do anything to black people" etc. etc. It is that history of racism that Michelle Obama was referencing when she said this is the first time that she's been proud of her country. For the white media to have taken her words and distorted them into some type of anti-patriotic vitriol is to continue to deny the reality of this country's bigoted, discriminatory and prejudicial history.

The reality is that America's deep history of racism reared its ugly head throughout the 2008 presidential election each time those petulant, whiny, talking heads on the cable news networks took something Obama said out of context and presented it to the public with a negative spin, designed to invoke fear and touch the basest instincts in those Americans who harbor hatred toward anyone whose skin is not white.

The reality is that whenever white America feels threatened by something or someone they don't understand or have little experience with, they respond with instinctive, historic racially motivated actions, words and/or tactics, the ultimate goal of which is to destroy the unknown. If they were being true to the tenets of the Christian religion they proclaim to believe so deeply in they would embrace the different, the unknown, the unfamiliar, so that when someone like Rush Limbaugh, Andrea Mitchell, Bill O'Reilly and many of the Fox News commentators, make statements to inflame the public, they can respond with disgust and demand an end to such biased and covertly racist reporting.

The reality is that in order for any of the above to take place, America must first pull its head out of its ass and **face** the reality that the revolution has already begun, if you look at what the Bush administration has done to the constitution…. How they have used it to establish dominance and control over not just the people of America, but throughout the world----this is a revolt and throughout history there has never been a bloodless revolt.

We can do a chronology of historical truth where wars were fought…usually because of disagreement between people; whether it is between 2 people or 2 million…I'm not talking about revolutions over establishing vegetarianism or over western influence of meat-eating during the 1600 hundreds… I am talking about when one form of government or group overthrows the other and its replacements, or when a sudden and momentous radical and extreme change in circumstances are brought upon a sect or group of people, not without bloodshed; to name a few: the Civil War, The Women's Suffrage Movement, The Revolutionary War, the Civil Rights Movement, the Underground Railroad, Unionization; hell!!! even South Africans' fight against Apartheid, genocide and ethnic cleansing as they call it… all represent a major shift in power and control, a changing of the status quo, and the ones in power who were being challenged, did not give up or share that power and control without someone's blood being spilled. Am I advocating that this revolution of which I speak will involve bloodshed?

Look at America's history! Do you have the guts to call for and participate in the revolution or are you willing to sit back and watch the empire fall?

Notes

1. J.A. Rogers. *The Five Negro Presidents: According to what White People Said They Were.* Published by Helga M. Rogers, St. Petersburg, FL 1965

CHAPTER **5**

The Revolution and I/We

An historic opportunity has been presented before America. The 2008 Presidential election was the time for *all* Americans to reclaim the government and place power back into the hands of the people as people abroad have done. It was the time to make the American government of the people, by the people and for the people. Washington had been taken over by the criminals, and the people had been removed from power. The political leaders and corporate owners, along with the "ten per centers" (the 10% who own 85% of the wealth in America) that actually run this country have had free rein to disregard law and order, here and abroad. They've committed crimes against the population in the pursuit of the almighty dollar and did so with impunity because they've constructed the laws so that the criminal is protected and the victim is persecuted.

The people of America have been terribly skewered by the pundits in Washington, who have the power to bring all these machinations out into the open, but instead, choose to harp on insignificant tidbits or make news where there is no news. In starting the revolution, the people of America first need to bring the media under our control and perhaps then, the truth can be reported. In order for America to be restored to some sense of decency from the incipient stages, to regain respectability from around the world morally and spiritually, a revolution has to take place.

This government as we know it, be we black or white, has a moral obligation to this nation to heal all that was lost from the slave trade to the Emancipation Proclamation; from George Washington to the president/dictator/"decision-maker" (Bush 43) of America and his cohorts. There was a time when the people spoke and their government listened. Up through and including the Bush (43) administration, Washington had been ignoring the people as well as the rest of the world; regardless of the displeasure America's allies expressed to the Bush administration, it came down on deaf ears. Dick Cheney expressed it succinctly when he responded "So?" in an interview where he was confronted with statistics that showed a majority of Americans were unhappy with the strain that the Iraq war was putting on this economy.

Barack started the charge for change with his presidential campaign. He brought in a whole new generation of voters, who heeded his call for change. This created a powerful base for his presidential run and his opponents knew it. So much so that his call for change was hijacked by several of his Democratic opponents, including Chris Dodd, John Edwards, Bill Richardson, Dennis Kucinich and even the formidable "I don't quit" Hillary Clinton. We even saw and heard John McCain calling for change and he started with himself. Every week when we saw him on the news, he'd reinvented himself, standing for something he was formerly against or speaking against something he stood for in the past. The people of America wanted the change that Barack stood for, they thirsted for it and Barack was the long drink of water that quenched that thirst. His election to the presidency will be the start of the people taking matters into their hands collectively to get a hold onto this government that is supposed to be of the people, by the people and for the people.

America needs a revolution to take back the government that was stolen by the Republicans starting with the 2000 election, which was achieved with the help of Florida's Republican Secretary of State, Katherine Harris—who also happened to be the co-chair of

Bush's election campaign in that state. They did it again in Ohio during the 2004 election, this time with the help of Republican Secretary of State Kenneth Blackwell, who also was the co-chair of Bush's re-election campaign in that state. A recurring theme?

As documented in the film *American Blackout* both Harris and Blackwell allegedly manipulated the outcome of election results by purging thousands of voters from the voting rolls, among other tactics.[1]

For instance, the film reports that both Harris and Blackwell falsely identified thousands of voters as felons and had their names removed from the voter rolls. Long after the election was over in Florida, it was discovered that a company called Database Technologies, the Florida division of ChoicePoint, Inc., had improperly scrubbed 57,700 legal voters off the Florida rolls, many of whom would have most likely voted for Vice President Al Gore (they were primarily Black Americans and traditionally, Blacks tend to vote for the democratic candidate.) ChoicePoint, now a LexisNexis-owned company, maintains databases of personal background information on virtually every consumer in America and sells that information to government agencies and private companies. Database Technologies was paid $2.3 million dollars (or $4.3 million, depending on the source) by The Florida Republicans in 2000 to compile their felony "scrub" list.

> "… DBT was hired, in part, to comb through computerized records around the country to identify former felons registered to vote in Florida. After wrongly identifying 8,000 Florida voters with Texas misdemeanor records as felons, it supplied a revised list of 57,770 "possible felons" to Florida's secretary of state, Katherine Harris."[2]

In a 2001 story produced by Newsnight, a BBC nightly news show, the Vice President of ChoicePoint, James Lee, told reporters that the Florida state government made it clear that it "wanted there to be more names than were actually verified as being a convicted felon."[3]

What's more, ChoicePoint had allegedly contributed large amounts of money to Republican candidates in 2000, leading to the observation that the company's error coincidentally benefited that party.

In Ohio, news outlets reported that over 300,000 voters were expunged from the rolls. In Cleveland alone, this amounted to nearly one in four names being removed between 2000 and 2004.[4] During the 2004 elections, Ohio voters were being told they could not vote in that election process because they didn't vote in the previous elections, according to Barbara Arnwine, Executive Director of the Lawyers Committee for Civil Rights Under Law, a nonprofit group formed in 1963 at the request of President John F. Kennedy to involve the private bar in providing legal services to address racial discrimination.

The film went on to document that in spite of unprecedented numbers of Democrats registering to vote in Ohio during the 2004 elections, voting machines were removed from predominately Black precincts, resulting in lines where some people waited in the rain for over 12 hours to cast their vote. Other improprieties in Ohio included people being told they couldn't vote because they were in the wrong precinct, even though they had voted in those same precincts in previous elections. In Ohio as in Florida, votes cast for the Democratic candidate were counted as votes for the Republican candidate, George Bush. In a posting on Rolling-Stone.com in June of 2006, Robert F. Kennedy, Jr. wrote:

> "...After carefully examining the evidence, I've become convinced that the president's party mounted a massive, coordinated campaign to subvert the will of the people in 2004. Across the country, Republican election officials and party stalwarts employed a wide range of illegal and unethical tactics to fix the election."[5]

Yet, in view of all the evidence and suspicious activity, the mainstream media, print and electronic, was strangely silent or dismissive; deriding those who spoke of the improprieties and doing nothing to question the validity of the election results, in 2000 or 2004. This is why it is no sad thing to see large, established, print media powerhouses fold and disappear. They say it is due to lack of advertising dollars and readership. Give the American citizenry some credit: they have recognized the uselessness of the print media and soon, too, of the electronic media.

The sad thing is, we will never know for sure if the 2004 Ohio election truly was stolen because, in spite of Ohio election law, the election ballots from 7 counties no longer exist and there are only partial records from 56 of the 88 counties. In 2007, election officials from the affected counties reported various reasons for the missing records, from being lost, misplaced, and damaged by water, to being taken to landfills -- all apparently by mistake, due to miscommunications, or because local election administrators said they were not aware of the state ballot preservation law (ballots must be preserved for 22 months beyond the day of the election) or the federal court order directing the preservation of the ballots due to several lawsuits that were filed.[6] I leave it to you the reader to draw your own conclusion as to what this means.

The presidential selection of 2001 was the next to last chance for America to save itself from the losing of its empire due to its refusal to stop the lying, cheating, stealing, killing, and the raping of this land and its American people. There is no honesty in Washington mainly because of the tyranny of Dick Cheney and George W. Bush 43, along with a host of the same old dinosaurs that served starting with the recycling of the Nixon administration, Gerald Ford, Ronald Reagan, George H.W. Bush 41, William Jefferson Clinton, and a repeat of the Bush Administration had John McCain won the general election over Barack Obama... speaking of which, how do you explain the Phoenix-like resurrection of John McCain's candidacy to front-runner?

Was the Republican election hi-jacking machine back at work?

In the 2008 presidential election, Republicans attempted to find a reason to negatively impact the process. When it was revealed that affiliates of the national organization ACORN had submitted falsified names on voter registration forms in Nevada, the Republicans jumped all over it as an Obama conspiracy to commit voter fraud and to combat it, called for implementation of "poll monitors" nationwide. What this amounted to was armed, uniformed underlings intimidating legitimate voters at the polls.

Granted, there was evidence that workers under certain ACORN-sponsored local organizations were in fact "registering" ghost voters; case in point, a friend of mine in St. Petersburg, FL received a letter from Pinellas County's Supervisor of Elections informing her that her registration form was rejected because the identification numbers didn't match state records. The fact that the name on the letter she received was the same as hers with the exception of the middle initial and had her current residential address raised suspicion and caused her to contact the county elections office.

After she insisted on speaking with the supervisor in charge of the office to determine how this occurred, it was discovered that a group called A Work in Progress had indeed submitted the falsified registration form. The question was raised as to whether there were other incidents that the Elections office was aware of and if so, what was being done to protect her and other citizens from being turned away at the polls or dropped from the active registered voter rolls. She was assured that her registration was intact and that the form submitted with the facsimile of her name would be destroyed and never added to the rolls because there were no matching identification numbers in state records.

When she asked who monitored these groups or whether

they were required to be certified or registered with any authority, she was astounded that the answer was no one monitored these groups and there were no registration requirements. She was referred to the state's voter fraud hotline to report the incident. The supervisor at the local elections supervisor's office informed her that their office would notify the state of Florida of the organization's activities.

All of this begs the question, how many legitimate voters received this same letter and didn't take any action? Did they face difficulty when they presented themselves at the polls on November 4th? It would have been very easy for Republicans to take advantage of situations like that to create doubt and provide Republican-led state elections offices with a reason to purge similar-sounding names of legitimate voters. Remember you heard it here first. America, you better be on the lookout 'cause ain't nobody else looking out for ya!

It is time for the revolution; not as most would want to believe (i.e. black against white), but transferring power to the people. Only then would we be able to suspend, or perhaps even avoid, the fall of America. However, we must act now and swiftly, recognizing that this is not a problem for black people or white people but a problem for all who call themselves American.

In this revolution where we must begin to take back our government, do you think the power mongers will stand down without a fight? Hardly; case in point…the 2000 and 2004 elections, and even the hate-mongering perpetrated during the 2008 election.

"When opportunity knocks" as they say open the door. In the booklet "The 5 Negro Presidents", J.A. Rogers wrote:

> "In 1963 when Attorney- General Kennedy and Senator Javits said there might be a black person as president in the next thirty or forty years, FACT, the most outspoken magazine of the time, replied that there was already one and, in its January/February 1964 issue, had an article

"America's First Negro President". It named Warren G. Harding as the one according to affidavits from elderly white people who had known the family."[7]

It has been 47 years since that statement was made, and throughout the 2008 presidential campaign, poll after poll read "Is America ready for a black president?" I posed the question is America ready for a female president? It's the mentality that creates polls such as these that lets us know America has serious problems to think that only a white male can be president and it doesn't matter how dumb he is! There was no poll to ask is America ready for a dumbass was there? No!... they just felt it was better to let a dumbass run the country and the world rather than somebody that really had some smarts about them , or rather than to let a woman or a Black man, in spite of their intelligence, have an opportunity.

Change IS gonna come...the revolution demands it. Rome was not built in a day and neither this country nor its government was built right the first time. If America wants to continue on this path of destruction by way of its dirty misdeeds, and overt disregard and mistreatment of the people of America, then ignore the call to heed for the atonement of America.

When you hear Americans talk about the United States of America, or the European Common Market, or the Commonwealth of Russia, they're not speaking of members of the dark world. This only means that all whites are united; that doesn't include members of the dark world (people of color).

When whites decide they really want to help, we will see them start organizations comprised of people of means to have discussions about how they can be a part of repairing the ill effects stemming from slavery and other acts of oppression. Characteristically, America makes agreements or sign treaties, then fails to honor those agreements (think the Native Americans). The revolution demands that there must be a change; stop the lip service, which is designed to distract the people from the tricks and lies perpetuated by the Bushits and the Dickless Cheneys that still impact America today.

If you believe a revolution is at hand, and really, truly want to help eradicate this problem, I challenge you to organize yourselves and include people of all races and creeds; after all it was you, White America that created this mess so it is incumbent upon you to fix it. As long as whites do not take it upon themselves to eradicate the climate they created, America will continue its moral decline.

Notes

1. Ian Inaba, Director. *American Blackout.* Guerrilla News Network, 2006 Video available on Vodpod.com http://vodpod.com/search/browse/?q=American+Blackout

2. Julian Borger and Gregory Palast. *Inquiry into new claims of poll abuses in Florida election.* The Guardian Unlimited, February 17, 2001. http://www.guardian.co.uk/world/2001/feb/17/usa.julianborger/

3. Ibid.

4. Robert F. Kennedy, Jr. *Was the 2004 Election Stolen?* Rolling Stone Magazine, 6/1/06 http://www.rollingstone.com/news/story/10432334/was_the_2004_election_stolen

5. Ibid.

6. Steven Rosenfeld. *In Violation of Federal Law, Ohio's 2004 Presidential Election Records Are Destroyed or Missing.* Alternet.org, July 30, 2007. http://www.alternet.org/story/58328

7. J.A. Rogers. *The Five Negro Presidents: According to what White People Said They Were.* Published by Helga M. Rogers, St. Petersburg, FL 1965

CHAPTER 6

The Empire's Stolen Economy

Speaking of hustlers…In America there is a group called the "ten per centers"; this is what is known as the financial elite or the wealthiest people in the nation who are even excluded from paying income tax as well as all other forms of taxes, simply because they have so much money. They allow other people to use their money as long as it does not find its way back to them for the avoidance of paying taxes. Avarice and greed are recognized in every religion as undesirable traits, but this capitalistic and morally bankrupt country thrive on them. Consider:

In 1933, Franklin D. Roosevelt said, "The real truth of the matter is that a financial element in the large centers has owned the government since the days of Andrew Jackson".

In 1944, Benjamin Disraeli, an English statesman, made the following statement: "The world is governed by very different personages from what is imagined by those who are not behind the scenes."

One reason given for the root cause of the Revolutionary War was that King George III of England outlawed the use of the interest-free currency the colonies were producing for themselves and forced them to borrow money from the Central Bank of England, with interest, which immediately put the colonies into debt. Benjamin Franklin wrote: "The refusal of King George III to allow the colonies to operate an honest money system, which freed the ordinary man from the clutches of money manipulators, was probably the prime cause of the Revolution."

Today, the ordinary man of America is held in the clutches of the money manipulators behind the Central Bank of this country better known as the Federal Reserve. The congressional act of creating the Fed was and remains unconstitutional according to Article 1, Section 8 of the Constitution. Typical of the thieves that run this economy, the act was passed on a day when most members of congress had left Washington for the Christmas holidays and the ones who did vote for it (that weren't on the committee that approved the act) hadn't read the bill and didn't know what it contained. The constitution gave limited powers to Congress regarding the creation and issuance of paper money, which, by the creation of the Federal Reserve system, they relinquished their responsibility and by extension, the power of the people of the United States, to a privately held corporation whose members are some of the wealthiest people in the world.

Most Americans don't know the history behind the Federal Reserve and believe it's a functioning department or division of the federal government while in reality, it's not. In truth it is a privately owned corporation that isn't controlled or regulated in any way by the federal government. To make it acceptable to the people, the buildings are designed to mimic the architecture of most federal buildings and that is one way the people are fooled. It controls the interest rates and inflation (money supply) of this nation. It produces and loans money at interest, to the government. How does the government pay back the loans...through the illegal collection of federal income taxes from working citizens of this country.

The collection of federal income taxes is unconstitutional because the 16th amendment was never legally ratified. Bill Benson, a former investigator with the Illinois Department of Revenue, has published a book titled *The Law That Never Was* which details his year long investigation of national and state archives regarding the proposed amendment. The constitution requires that the legislatures of 3/4ths of the states of the US ratify a proposed amendment in order for it to be added to the constitution. In 1913 when the amendment was supposedly ratified, there were 48 states in the union, which meant that 36 states had to approve it. Benson's research revealed that the Secretary of State, Philander Knox, proclaimed 38 states had ratified the 16th amendment when he had documentation that 11 states had failed to vote on the amendment, Kentucky had rejected the amendment, Minnesota never sent in any documentation of a vote, and 33 states changed the language of the amendment, an act that is prohibited by the Constitution.[1]

Forty percent of our illegally collected personal federal income taxes go towards paying the interest on the debt created by the US government. Where do the working citizens get the money to pay income taxes? From the Central Bank (Federal Reserve) which produces new "money" that it loans at interest to member banks who then loan money to the businesses that withholds the taxes from your earnings…that money goes directly into the pockets of the private (and foreign) owners of the Federal Reserve, as a *guaranteed and required* 6% annual tax-free PROFIT in the form of dividends. The profit comes because the paper they used to print the money costs next to nothing and the fees they pay to the US Bureau of Printing and Engraving is less than 3 cents for every $100 printed. Although there is a law that requires all profits minus expenses and salaries to be returned to the US Treasury, neither Congress nor the IRS have the power to audit the Fed, so no one really knows exactly how much money they collect!

The Federal Reserve has the power to regulate the value of the currency in the United States by increasing and decreasing the supply of money. By virtue of the fact that the member banks which actually "own" the fed are in turn owned by foreigners, our economy is at the mercy of these foreigners and they can cause it to collapse anytime they wish simply by "creating" and circulating more money than there are goods and services. This is called inflation.

The most important thing for you citizens of America to understand is that the purpose of this "scam" is to produce DEBT. Every dollar that is produced (manufactured out of thin air) by the Federal Reserve equals immediate debt because it is loaned to the federal government with interest. We need to demand that our legislators abolish the Fed or buy it back!

Thomas Jefferson said "Banking institutions, paper money, and paper speculation are capable of undermining the nation's stability ... The Constitution does not empower the Congress to establish a National Bank. Rather than trust the nation's currency to private hands, the circulating medium should be restored to the nation itself to whom it belongs."[2]

Another Jefferson quote "...if the American people ever allow private banks to control the issue of currency...the banks and corporations that will grow up around them will deprive people of their property until their children wake up homeless on the continent their fathers conquered." [3] Prophetic sign of the times wouldn't you say?

Sir Josiah Stamp, an English economist who was president of the Bank of England in the 1920's and reputed to be the 2nd richest man in England, is often attributed with this quote: "Banking was conceived in iniquity and was born in sin. The Bankers own the earth. Take it away from them, but leave them the power to create deposits (money), and with the flick of the pen they will create enough deposits (money) to buy it back again. However, take it away from them, and all the great fortunes like mine will disappear and they ought to disappear, for this would be a happier and better world to live in. But, if you wish to remain the slaves of Bankers and pay the cost of your own slavery, let them continue to create deposits (money)." [4]

The following is an excerpt from an article written by Stephen

Lendman, a contributing author to Global Research.com regarding the Federal Reserve:

> "The Fed harms the public welfare in one other important way, and again most people are none the wiser about it. Supposedly the Federal Reserve System was established to stabilize the economy, smooth out the business cycle, maintain a healthy rate of sustainable growth while holding prices steady and benefitting everyone. So how well has it done its job? Since its creation in 1913, and with them in charge, we had the crashes of 1921 and the most important and remembered one in 1929. That was followed by The Great Depression which lasted until the onset of WW II that noted conservative economist Milton Friedman explained was caused and exacerbated because the Federal Reserve oddly decided to reduce the money supply at a time of economic contraction instead of increasing it.

> "We then had recessions in 1953, 1957, 1969, 1975, 1981, 1990 and 2001. We also had inflation beginning in the 1960s which became quite severe through much of the 1970s and early 1980s. And we had a major banking crisis in the 1980s at which time more banks and savings and loan associations failed than ever before in our history. It happened in the wake of financial market deregulation when banks were allowed to pursue their own interests without government oversight to check their willingness to assume excess risk or stop them from trying to get away with deliberate fraud.

> "Along with the economic stability the Fed never achieved, we've also had:
> - soaring consumer debt
> - record high federal budget and trade deficits

- a high level of personal bankruptcies and rising mortgage loan delinquencies
- interest on a mounting national debt that's a large and rising percentage of the federal budget
- the loss of our manufacturing base and it's high-paying jobs with good benefits because they're being exported to low wage countries
- an economy in which services now account for nearly 80% of all business that provide mostly lower paying, less skilled jobs with few or no benefits, and
- a widening income and wealth gap that continues to harm lower and middle income earners to benefit the rich and privileged few and a government that encourages it"[5]

Now that the scoundrels have been exposed, what are you gonna do about it, America? A revolution requires revolutionary thinking and actions. I suggest you begin by refusing to play the game any longer, i.e., refuse to line the pockets of the money manipulators by refusing to pay federal income taxes, for one. As your Christian bible says, when you have a quarrel with your neighbor, you are to go to him and if he refuses to hear you, you are to go public. Shout down the congressmen holding town hall meetings and show up with your guns, like you did over health-care reform and insist that they rescind the authority given to the Federal Reserve. Return that power to the elected body which is supposed to represent the people. As Carter G. Woodson said: "Each one, teach one"; therefore, question the authority for you now know that it's corrupt and they are only interested in your INTEREST! Refuse to contribute to the building of a weapon that is being used to destroy you, your children, and your grandchildren. The colonists had the guts to start a revolution to end a foreign government's control of the economy, so what's your excuse today, America?

Notes

1. Bill Benson. http://www.thelawthatneverwas.com/new/home.asp

2. Lipscomb and Bergh, Editors. *The Writings of Thomas Jefferson,* Memorial Edition http://www.etext.virginia.edu

3. Ibid.

4. Liberty-Tree.ca
    http://quotes.liberty-tree.ca/quotes_by/sir+Josiah+stamp

5. Stephen Lendman. *The Federal Reserve.* Posted June 29, 2006. Z-Net : The Spirit of Resistance Lives http:www.zmag.org/znet/viewarticle/3649

CHAPTER 7

When in Rome...

As noted earlier, America's decline closely resembles that of the Roman Empire. Its government was full of corrupt leaders and the people paid little attention to the goings-on. Here in America, our government is full of corrupt leaders elected to office, and we pay little attention to how much they steal from us with the passing of every bill.

A revolution is multi-faceted and as such, those participating in the revolution have to take a variety of steps to take back their government. One such step is to put a stop to the corrupt financial wrangling that goes on in the Congress, specifically, the earmarks that certain Republican (as well as Democratic) congressmen (and women), push through Congress that enrich their bank accounts at the expense of the American people. Of 24 congressmen and women identified by The Citizens for Responsibility in Ethics in Washington (CREW) as the most corrupt, 7 were Democrats.[1] They made the list not just for financial corruption but moral corruption as well (remember Larry Craig and David Vitter).

In August of 2008, FOXNEWS broadcast a story about the financial gain of certain members of Congress through earmarks attached, sometimes secretly, to bills being considered by Congress. Specifically reported on were Republican Representative (CA) Ken Calvert and Democratic Representative (PA) Paul Kanjorski, who pushed through earmarks that were designed specifically to benefit themselves or members of their families under the guise of bringing jobs or technology to their districts.[2] Calvert was on CREWs most corrupt list in 2006, 2007 and 2008.

According to the broadcast, and the report by CREW, Rep. Calvert, formerly a California real estate professional, and his partner paid $550,000 for a 4 acre piece of land in Perris, CA in 2005. This property was 4 miles south of the March Air Reserve Base. In less than a year, without making any improvements to the land, they sold the property for $985,000; a $435,000 profit. During this same period Calvert pushed through an earmark to a bill which secured 8 million dollars for an overhaul and expansion of a freeway interchange 16 miles from the property as well as an additional 1.5 million dollars for commercial development in the same area around the airfield, the result of which was an increase in the value of his property and his personal wealth.

He continued his involvement with an investment group who purchased property a few blocks from the proposed interchange. Within 6 months after the earmark for the interchange was appropriated, the property that was purchased for $975,000 was then sold for 1.45 million dollars. Calvert's real estate firm received a commission on this sale. By using his position to push through earmarks that advanced his own financial interests, Calvert's actions were a direct violation of Congress's ban on using congressional positions for personal financial gain. In May of 2007, Calvert was brought before the Congressional Ethics Committee for his role in pushing through a $5.6 million earmark for a transit center less than 4 miles from 6 properties that he owned, which he purchased in 2004 for between $250,000 and $500,000. After the earmark went through that same property was sold for between 100,000 and 1 million dollars according to Calvert's financial disclosure in 2006. The committee determined that his actions were not a conflict of interest because *he was not the sole beneficiary of the transactions!*

In the same August 2008 FOXNEWS report, Rep. Kanjorski's actions were perhaps the most blatantly unethical and criminal. The earmarks he requested took taxpayer dollars and directly deposited them into his personal bank account and/or those of immediate family members.

The report revealed how Kanjorski recommended a personal friend, John Yudichak, to run a non-profit organization to refurbish surplus government construction equipment and use it for reclamation projects. According to the FOXNEWS report, in 1998, Kanjorski secured an earmark for 1.1 million dollars of federal money for the refurbishing non-profit to develop the use of water jet technology for pulverizing tires and energizing his district's coal industry.

Once the nonprofit had received the funds, Kanjorski came to Yudichak and told him that they did not have the expertise to develop the water jet technology, and he wanted them to partner with another company. That company, Cornerstone Technology, turned out to be owned and operated by Kanjorski's 4 nephews and daughter.

When Yudichak realized that all of the funds they had received from the federal government were to be turned over to this company, he threw Kanjorski's nephew Peter out of his office and refused to sign the contract he had brought with him. Yudichak then called a board meeting and urged the members to not accept the grant money and return it to the federal government. Kanjorski reportedly became enraged and adamantly told the board that they *would* accept that money. After the board meeting, Kanjorski confronted Yudichak and told him that they were "making him look bad and keeping him from taking care of his family".

He also reportedly threatened "to bury him (Yudichak) and would make sure his life would be ruined" if the non-profit did not accept the grant money. Kanjorski further threatened that the project would go through with or without the non-profit's cooperation.

As a final act of determination, the non-profit wrote a letter to the federal government informing them that the grant money was being refused.

In retribution, Kanjorski redirected the 1.1 million of grant money to the technology company set up by his family members. Since Yudichak considered himself a personal friend of Kanjorski's, he tried to restore some since of integrity to Kanjorski, (and Washington), but failed, as Kanjorski was able to direct another 9 million dollars of taxpayer money directly to the for-profit technology company set up by his 4 nephews and his daughter.

The building that the company originally operated out of was co-owned by Kanjorski and the rent checks went from the taxpayers' wallets directly into Kanjorski's personal bank account.

None of that money earmarked to Cornerstone was ever used to the benefit of the community Kanjorski represented and the company eventually went bankrupt, not having to repay one dime to their creditors (or the taxpayers).[3]

Congress has been earmarking taxpayer dollars for decades, many of which straddle the fine line between ethical and unethical, if not downright legal and illegal. Whenever questions arise about any such earmarks, the Congressional Ethics Committee is supposed to review the specifics and make a ruling as to the ethicality of the action. This is akin to having the fox guarding the henhouse.

If the American people refuse to send tax dollars to the federal government, we can make a direct impact on the availability of money for pork barrel projects that enrich the very ones that are supposed to be representing our best interests.

It is time for the revolution!

Notes

1. Citizens for Responsibility and Ethics in Washington (CREW). *CREW's Most Corrupt: Rep Ken Calvert* http://www.crewsmostcorrupt.org/summaries/calvert.php

2. FoxNews. *Porked: Earmarked for Profit.* Video broadcast 8/2008

3. Ibid.

CHAPTER 8

A Declining Educational System

An empire is only as strong as its people and without an educated people an empire is bound to fail. It's a bad thing when we have third world conditions right here in America. Let's consider the problem of our education system because, within neighborhoods children of all colors are increasingly looked upon as warehouse baggage that has accumulated, and now needs to be put out; this is the result of neglect and under-utilization, disparate impact, adverse impact, racism, and all the other sicknesses that live in America.

In 1906 Upton Sinclair wrote an astounding novel that shocked the meat packing industry about the conditions that existed that ultimately caused the health department to organize a safety and regulatory agency to oversee and set standards for how things should and should not be done. Jonathan Kozol sparked that same kind of atmosphere in the educational arena with his searing look at educational inequities in suburban and inner city America, discussed in his book Savage Inequalities. But in spite of his raw, naked and undiluted exposure of the inequities (read: financial funding) in the American public education system, the outrage is falling on deaf ears.

We have an education system that is on failure and that's a fact. Being an educator and running in those circles, I have worked with and encountered countless educational experts and specialists who were trying to develop a better way to educate America's children. However, there is a continued lack of support from the top. No matter how educated teachers are, they can only do what the "higher ups" dictate they can do. Education is the only professional field that is not regulated by its professionals; i.e., doctors are regulated by other doctors, lawyers are regulated by other lawyers, etc.; that and a multitude of other factors, such as substandard facilities, politicians refusing to fund certain programs, and legislating unfunded mandates such as No Child Left Behind, keep teachers from accomplishing the task for which they trained.

This is not by accident either, but rather by design. The American educational system is designed to ensure the continuation of the class system in this society. Certain groups of people HAVE to fail to be educated. Think about it, they come out of school uneducated which leads to a failure to be employed. In order for this capitalistic system to continue to flourish, there has to be a permanent underclass of people who are unemployed or underemployed!

We are producing a generation of educated illiterates...our children cannot READ, they cannot WRITE , they cannot THINK CRITICALLY, they cannot apply MATHEMATICAL concepts, hell, they can't even do basic computations without the aid of calculators! All you have to do is look at the statistics nationwide and compare them to when our generation was in school.

The American education system is suffering from intellectual tyranny. Mindlessness, recklessness, betrayal, exploitation are generally terms you associate with the penal system. However, these same terms are descriptive of America's academic institutions (or asylums). It is a broken system and no one from the inside is trying to fix it, not the educators, not the parents, not the students. American children are not being taught to be independent thinkers despite the oft-listed curriculum goal of "creating critical thinkers". If students were really being taught to be critical and independent thinkers, I believe the first thing they would question is the relevancy of what they're being force-fed as education.

Our generation and generations before us were raised to believe that education was the key to a secure (financially) future. We teach our children that they must get a high school diploma so they can go to college so they can get a job in corporate America and live the American dream. It was what we (well, some of us, anyway) did, it was what our parents did; it was right for them, it was right for us and therefore, it is right for our children.

The problem with this scenario is that the times and economic landscape have changed; corporate America doesn't exist anymore. There's no such thing as a secure future with a secure company because nothing is secure in America right now.

An educational revolution has to take place and it has to start with those who are charged with carrying it out...the teachers, the parents, the students. But before that can happen, their eyes must first be opened to the reality of the broken system. Education is not about learning to "get ahead"; it is not about making sure you can count 1-2-3 and say a-b-c; it's about "learning so you can pay me".

In this capitalist society, education is about gaining the skills necessary to become a "productive member of the middle class" by becoming employed in order to make someone else's dreams come true!

But those dreams are fast becoming a nightmare.

Across this country, state after state has implemented one form or another of high-stakes standardized testing, supposedly to make educators accountable as well as to raise the standards for graduation so our children can be competitive in the global market. In reality, the opposite occurs. What results is a subclass of people who are undereducated and underemployed because the vast majorities who don't pass the tests don't get a high school diploma and therefore don't go on to college or pursue any type of postsecondary education or training. The majority of this majority is predominately minorities, in particular Black males.

However, even among those who do manage to pass these tests and go on to college, many are unprepared for the demands of college level curriculums, requiring remediation in reading, writing and arithmetic. Of these, the completion rate for a two- or four-year degree is abysmal for an advanced superpower like America, and the numbers are declining each year.

According to the 2008 National Report Card issued by the National Center for Public Policy and Higher Education, America ranks sixth among developed nations with only 34% of young adults ages 18-24 enrolled in college. Korea ranks number one with 53%! The completion rate is even lower; America ranks 15th with only 18% of students completing certificate or degree programs. Australia, Japan and Switzerland are at the top of the heap with a 26% completion rate. When looking at the workforce, only 39% of American adults ages 25-34 have two year degrees or higher, compared to number one Canada, with 55%. Eight other countries have rates higher than America.[1]

The consequence of these numbers is a steadily declining pool of skilled and educated workers, reducing America's ability to remain competitive in the global market. In order to stay ahead of the game, you have to be a leader, and America is no longer ahead of its international competition with regards to an educated workforce.

The politicians that make and enforce the laws eventually have to be replaced. The engineers, who design new technology to improve our quality of life, eventually have to be replaced. The military men and women who operate the sophisticated weaponry that "keeps our country safe", eventually have to be replaced (especially at the rate they're being killed in Iraq, Afghanistan and at home once they return.) Somebody has to repair the bridges and roads, build and fly the airplanes and continue to teach in the broken system. The thousands of retiring Baby Boomers need workers to contribute to the Social Security pot they are depending upon for a source of income.

Where will they come from? Our children are dropping out mentally before they drop out physically and this is happening earlier and earlier in their school career. An educational revolution is the answer to this problem. An empire is only as strong as its weakest link and an educated populace is a necessity to maintain an economy and global dominance.

Notes

National Center for Public Policy and Higher Education. *Measuring Up 2008.* http://measuringup2008.highereducation.org

CHAPTER 9

Hypocritical Imperialism of an Empire in Decline

The dissention America has perpetrated and perpetuated around the world as "peacekeepers" and nation-builders, did not keep peace but incited conflict and reckless behavior as other countries welcomed America to establish embassies all over the world. The government organizations (GOs) and non-government organizations (NGOS), serve as spy organizations, put in place to keep tabs on what everybody is doing other than those that represent the selfish interests of America.

The United States' imperialism in the Middle East has always been raw, naked and undiluted, through tricknology, or definitively: the science of tricks and lies; with those traits comes a responsibility for maintaining and trying to keep U.S. power and control in that region through support of oppressive and dictatorial regimes which must be done in order to rule by hypocritical manipulation and anything else that re-energizes the whole founding principles on what defines America as America.

US imperialism in the Middle East is not imperialism in the usual sense of the word. There are no outward, direct government entities administered by the US as in, say Guam. Instead, they use surrogates like Saudi Arabia and Israel to wield its power; power that is purchased with arms and unconditional aid. The hypocrisy is that at one time they also used Iraq and Iran, both of whom are now considered "enemy states"; they support a country like Kuwait that still does not allow its women to vote and make no demands on Saudi Arabia to loosen its oppressive rule against its people.

What the United States has done in other places around the world is create dissention and confusion among everybody in order to take control over what doesn't rightfully belong to them, and it is very skillfully done, very cunning and crafty with deliberation, calculation and cruelty. A prime example is how the US government uses Israel to fight proxy wars with its Arab neighbors to curb any rise in Arab nationalism that may lead to loss of US control over Middle Eastern oil.

The US supplies Israel with weaponry, training, and money, to the tune of billions of dollars annually, and unlike aid provided to other sovereign nations, there are no strings attached or conditions related to how the money is to be spent, or what changes they are expected to institute, either in their style of government, or services rendered to the citizenry. Israel has been set up by the US to be the bully of the Middle East, not because the US can't assume the role themselves, but because to do so would be contrary to the calculating, cunning and crafty machinations that all U.S. administrations have operated under. As Dilip Hiro said: "It is much simpler to manipulate a few ruling families than a wide variety of personalities and policies bound to be thrown up by a democratic system."[1] If the U.S. intends to maintain its position in the world as viewed from the outside inward, America has to continue in that deceitful vein and tryst of lies to prevent its overthrow.

What else is to be expected when you have chosen to build your empire on the backs of a sect of people? As G_D said you should not build your kingdom on the backs of men, and this is what America has done… But you see there is some cynicism behind it all, because it is not for the good of the people in other parts of the world. In this world, there are a lot of people…unfortunately in

America they are split into groups called well-meaning-folks and not-so-well-meaning folks. The people who are making the major political, life-changing decisions for Americans are comprised of the not-so-well-meaning ones and that is not good.

It is good to be on the top, but when you get there through ill means and trickery, senseless murder, oppression, enslavement, rape, robbery, and all that is consistent with the history of America and how it rose to power, (which, by the way, was done under the guise of Christianity) you can't expect to stay there without facing a challenge from without.

The U.S. has always used disagreeably precise, penetrating tactics to carry out their agenda in an overly strict, inhibiting and disciplined manner to do its dirty deeds with inclusivity of the CIA and their same old strategic methods of blunder they use to in-filtrate, kill, steal and destroy at all costs. This has not gone un-noticed by Middle Eastern countries like Iran, who has boldly and defiantly told the U.S. to stay out of Iranian business (with regard to its nuclear program).

There are some real issues that need to be addressed regard-ing America's relationship with Africa in this twenty first century. America is the richest country in the world and sub-Saharan Africa continues to be among the poorest, with a per capita income av-eraging one US dollar per day. According to the United Nations Human Development report in 2007, the people of sub-Saharan Africa will make up more than 1/3 of the world's poorest people by 2015. How could this be so with the billions of dollars in aid that has been flowing into Africa since 1947? I'll tell you how; it is by design.

The United States has had a presence in Africa for nearly sev-enty five years on what this government likes to call peacekeeping missions; but Africans are dying in the same record numbers today as they have in the past. Under the watchful eye of United States' influence, apartheid was allowed to flourish and hunger was one of the leading causes of death. America needs to keep Africa in a subordinate position in order to take Africa's resources as its own. Instead of helping Africa to use its natural resources to benefit the African people, America and its allies have turned Africa into their own personal grocery store. They have raped the continent repeatedly, creating deep scars in their collective subconscious, using the billions of dollars in development money as a salve.

It brings to mind the biblical parable *Give a man a fish, he will eat for a day; teach a man to fish, he will eat forever*...the only problem in applying it to America's treatment of Africa, is that America has no intention of helping Africa feed itself. The proof is in the numbers; Africa is worse off today than it was 40 years ago. There is still abject poverty, staggering illiteracy and woefully inadequate medical care.

Instead of positioning its self to take control of Africa's oil resources for its own selfish reasons, America should be assisting Africa's nations with building schools, hospitals, healthcare facilities, and centers of manufacturing that would provide jobs for the citizens and an income stream for the government. If America was acting righteously in its revered Christianity, it would be working to bring Africa's nations together in statehood, to become a United States of Africa, teaching and training Africans how to govern themselves and utilize their natural resources as sources of income for the benefit of everyone. But, America would much rather enrich the already greedy and despotic leaders of the African nations in exchange for unilateral control of how their nation's resources are utilized to America's advantage, or in other words, creating pain for the African people while creating pleasure for themselves.

The nations of sub-Saharan Africa have little means of being self-sufficient, including the lack of a tax base to create a stream of income for the governments. The citizens of these African nations have no ownership of property or land, nothing of value, not even the little shanties in the townships of South Africa. Perhaps if they had ownership, then they'd have a source of collateral that would give them economic strength, which would then bring about political clout, which in turn establishes a voice.

When we look at Africa we can get a general idea of the overall direction in which the relationship between Africa and America is going. This is the measure for how the rest of world can determine its future in doing business with America and at what cost. The rest of the world needs to take a closer look at the inequalities that have helped shape America's wealth, for it is those that have made the U.S. the richest country in the world. These inequalities began with the eradication of the Native American Indian and the enslavement, genocide and rape of Africa and African people.

Africa is the victim of the greatest atrocity ever perpetrated against humanity; greater even than the supposed Holocaust and I say that without fear of contradiction; Poland, Germany and France were saved from total destruction and received the generosity and sympathy of other nations, America included, to become independent and self-sustaining nations. Africa has not been so fortunate…it has in fact, been set on auto-pilot for destruction from within. The pandemic of HIV/AIDS is a terror that has been perpetrated on the African people and their continent, engineered by America and her allies in the World Bank and International Monetary Fund as part of her grand scheme of attaining global hegemony.

The policies of America with regard to Africa should serve as a window on its intentions to eradicate Africa, or at the least, to marginalize its role on the international stage.

The American government has learned a valuable lesson from the war in Iraq. Had they said it was for humanitarian reasons to eliminate Saddam Hussein, they would have gotten the support of the American people. But having lied about weapons of mass destruction and sold the American people a bill of goods, they can't invade another country under the same guise.

The United States has already put its wheels in motion for war in Africa since the recent discovery of oil in the West African Gulf of Guinea. Analysts predict that the production of oil in that region in the coming years will rival the production of oil in all of the Persian Gulf. After the attacks of September 11, Colin Powell stated in US News that Africa had "strategic value to America". Although he was referencing the inclusion of African nations as allies in the war on terror, the real meaning was because of the tremendous oil reserves found there.

To prove my point: in 2001, then-Vice President Dick Cheney issued his energy policy in which he confirmed that Africa would be one of the fastest growing sources for oil and gas for the United States.[2] This was further reiterated in February 2002 by Walter Kansteiner, who at the time was the Assistant Secretary of State for African Affairs, when he described African oil as an "appealing national strategy for the United States".[3]

Further evidence of America's real intentions towards Africa is brought to light in a Congressional Research Service report for Congress issued in December of 2007. According to the report, which addresses "US Strategic Interests and the Role of the Military in Africa", analysts and policymakers in recent years, have stressed Africa's growing strategic importance to US interests. The report gave a list of these interests, which I liken to the list of ingredients manufacturers are required to put on their processed foods, which must list those ingredients in order from the most to the least. The higher the ingredient is on the list, the higher the concentration of that ingredient in the food product.

Similarly, the list of interests in the CRS report placed the importance of Africa's natural resources, particularly its energy resources, as 2nd on the list, ahead of concern for humanitarian crises, including HIV/AIDS. More evidence: the report goes on to state that Africa has surpassed the Middle East as the largest supplier of crude oil to the United States, "further emphasizing the continent's strategic importance"[4]. In fact, according to Jason Motlagh's article, *America's Africorps*, in 2006, Nigeria was the fifth-largest supplier of oil to the US...and analysts predicted that by 2010, the Gulf of Guinea would be supplying 25% of

America's crude oil, more than what is supplied by Saudi Arabia.[5] (Note: According to the Department of Energy's Energy Information Administration, Africa recently surpassed the Middle East as America's largest supplier of crude oil).

According to an April 2003 article by Suraya Dadoo titled *When Uncle Sam Comes Calling in Africa,* Nigeria, the largest producer and exporter of oil in Africa, has pumped over $300 billion dollars worth of oil over the last 40 years, but 70% of its population continued to live on less than $1 a day, in spite of the Nigerian government collecting an estimated $14 billion a year in oil revenue. To quote Stanford University political scientist Terry Lynn Karl in the same article, "We don't have a single example of oil leading to long term positive outcomes in developing countries."[6] Dadoo notes that the US oil company Exxon stood to earn almost $4.6 billion dollars from Africa's largest oil project, the Chad-Cameroon pipeline, a project that has been the subject of criticism for its environmental damage and the fact that there is no accountability on the part of Exxon or the two countries as to how much money these countries stand to gain from this pipeline. Without this documentation, the very people who should be benefitting from such a venture have no way to hold their governments accountable.

The bulk of the CRS report outlines the role of the American military on the continent. It should be noted that when the US designates something as being a strategic national interest, it "reserves the use of force to secure and defend such interests if necessary."[7]

The 2007 CRS report went into detail about the unified combatant command announced by the Bush Administration in February of 2007 referred to as AFRICOM. The announced purpose of AFRICOM (US Africa Command) is to promote US national security objectives in Africa and its surrounding waters, by working with African nations (which ones?) and regional organizations (not identified in the report) to strengthen stability and security in the region. Military training and equipment is to be provided to the security forces of struggling African nations with ungoverned or uncontrolled spaces, caused primarily by political instability and civil war. When crises erupt in these areas, AFRICOM would be directed by national (American) command authorities to use its military operations to deter aggression.[8] The deterrence, mind you, would not be for the protection of the African people, but for the protection of America's "strategic interests" in Africa's oil reserves.

Herein lays the irony: every oil-rich nation in Africa that has established ties with America is engaged in civil war, or is led by corrupt leaders, with its people living in abject poverty. It would seem that US intervention increases the political and social tensions rather than resolves the longstanding conflicts. The millions of dollars that are being generated through the extraction of oil are going into the pockets of the extremist government leaders of those countries and the corporate boardrooms of the oil companies.

It's a safe bet to say that the increased American military presence in Africa has a hidden agenda: to position the US in a military confrontation with China over Africa's oil reserves. Already a commercial giant, China gets an estimated 30% of its crude oil from Africa[9] and is concentrating on and continuing its aim to be the world's next super power; and, when asked in 2003 by Political Affairs Magazine where the next oil conflict might be, Michael Klare, the author of Resource Wars, replied "I think in Africa, the situation there is heating up."[10] As a matter of fact, in a BBC News report from October 2008, reporter Adam Mynott wrote that America's need to counter the growing influence of China on the African continent was one of three reasons for the unification of Africom.[11]

With its insatiable appetite for energy and natural resources to fuel its booming growth and development, coupled with its 1.3 trillion, predominately US dollar reserves, China is actively engaging in a geopolitical "gotcha"!

Unlike the United States and its World Bank allies, China is wooing African leaders with their no-strings-attached soft money loans and cancelled debt. While the World Bank and the International Monetary Fund (IMF) hamstring African nations with "structural adjustment programs" that essentially allows them to micromanage the economies of the borrowing nations, China provides funds and manpower for rebuilding the infrastructure of countries like Angola, Zambia, Sudan and Nigeria, without interfering with how these governments operate. What China gets in exchange for its generosity is almost exclusive access to the oil exports of these nations, as well as non-oil commodities such as iron ore, copper, nickel, platinum and cobalt.

Of course, this drives the bureaucrats in Washington mad beyond all definition and has led to the strange accusation that China is trying to "secure oil at the sources", something Washington foreign policy has been preoccupied with for decades.[12]

Yet, in spite of the positive impact that China's investment may be having on African economies and infrastructures, there is still the problem of Africa's resources being removed for the benefit of other nations. Yes, schools and hospitals are being built, roads and bridges are being repaired, irrigation systems are being developed, but self-sufficiency will not be a result of these projects. The raping of Africa continues, even under the auspices of good deeds, like those above. On the surface, it appears that China is helping Africa more so than America and her allies, but when you look at things in their rightful perspective, China has imposed a form of slavery upon the people of the African countries where they do business. In the factories that are built by the Chinese the top paying jobs go to Chinese nationals while the Africans are employed at low wages to create the products that China then sells on the open market; sounds like the sweat shops that American manufacturers have set up in China! I question why they're not being trained in the skilled work so they can form companies of their own and bid on these same projects, keeping the wealth within the country. China doesn't do it and neither does America nor her cohort countries.

Like the Tanzam Railway built by the Chinese in the 1970's, without the income and skilled workers to provide the required maintenance, these projects will eventually fall into a sad state of disrepair. After all, it is Chinese-owned engineering and construction firms responsible for building the projects and those owners and their project managers leave the country once the projects are completed. The loans and grants provided to these African nations are not used to provide training programs for the African workers, nor are any provided as start-up funds for African-owned construction and engineering firms. It angers me that the leaders of these nations don't insist that anyone who wants to extract the natural resources must provide education, job training and factories for manufacturing so they won't be dependent upon outside "developmental aid". It further angers me that these same leaders use the revenues they receive from the extraction of their natural resources not for the benefit of the people they lead, but to enrich themselves and their cronies, or to pay for armed conflict against their own people.

In order for Africa to be a real player in the dynamics of world trade, these things have to be done unselfishly and that can only be achieved by disrupting the present system and giving the power to the people of Africa to determine the direction their country is going. The people of Africa need to play significant roles in policy making while understanding the importance of who, what, when, where, how and why of political hoopla concerning the natural resources of its continent.

The problem with this is there are no defining or conclusive directives with regards to the African people as far as inclusion. The U.S. should be willing to assist Africa in becoming the United States of Africa as they did in helping Russia become a commonwealth and Europe establish the European Common Market. Only then can they begin the process of doing business by working with the African nations and regional organizations to help strengthen, stabilize and perhaps secure areas that have been educated enough to understand the process in which to grow. If military might is needed in the areas that cannot be stabilized through diplomacy, then the structure is there to establish GOs and NGOs by creating jobs and industry as a united development. With the most recent discovery of oil being second to none, it should be more than enough for Africa's states to compete globally in the world market of supply and demand. Given this economic base, the African states could maintain their sovereignty and be in a position to repel any attempts by America or any other country to lay claim to their rich reserves of oil.

Don't be fooled: America's interests abroad are not humanitarian. As Bill Clinton would have said, "It's the oil, stupid."

Notes

1. Paul D'Amato. *U.S. Intervention in the Middle East: Blood for Oil*. International Socialist Review Online Edition. Issue 15, December 2000 – January 2001

2. Joaquin Oramas. *Oil, the Only U.S. Interest in Africa*. Political Affairs Magazine Online Edition July – August 2005 http://politicalaffairs.net/article/view/1487/1/108

3. Ibid.

4. Lauren Ploch. CRS Report RL 34003. *Africa Command: U.S. Strategic Interests and the Role of the Military in Africa*. Congressional Research Service Issued December 7, 2007

5. Jason Motlagh. *America's AfricaCorps*. AsiaTimes Online 9/21/2006 http://www.atimes.com   Retrieved 12/26/2006

6. Suraya Dadoo. *When Uncle Sam comes calling in Africa*. Znet online magazine. Posted 4/30/2003 http://www.zmag.org/content/showarticle.ctm   Retrieved 12/26/2006

7. Motlagh.

8. Ploch.

9. F. William Engdahl. *China and USA in New Cold War over Africa's Oil Riches*. Global Research Posted May 20, 2007   http://globalresearch.ca/printarticle.php   Retrieved 4/16/208

10. Oramas.

11. Adam Mynott. *U.S. Africa Command Battles Skeptics*. Posted on BBC News 10/1/2008 http://newsvote.bbc.co.uk/mpapps/pagetools/print/news Retrieved 10/5/2008

12. Engdahl

Afterword

We started this book during the last year of the Bush Administration with the intent of sounding a wake-up call to the people of this country to pay attention to the declining moral, cultural and spiritual character of America. Much was going on that no one, particularly the mainstream media, was paying attention to. We found it odd that we could tune in to the BBC and hear news stories *about* America that were not being reported *in* America. There is no substance to what passes as news today and the American people don't question the shallowness of it all. This apathetic attitude of Americans is a contributing factor to the decay of this country.

This country has an ugly past, one that started with deceit, prejudice, racism and oppression. When a lie is told, another lie has to be told to cover up the first lie, and then another lie has to be told to cover up the second lie, until so many lies have been told to the point that you're no longer dealing with reality. Reality is something this country does not like to deal with. Even the late George Carlin joked about how Americans don't like to hear the truth; they like to use euphemisms and soft language because they can't deal with reality. We believe in presenting the raw, naked and undiluted truth.

Most Americans believe there is nothing that can be done to change the direction the country's headed…that one person can't make a difference. Nothing could be further from the truth…but change won't happen if we just sit back and wait for the other guy to solve the problem. No societal change has ever taken place without a revolution from the people being oppressed and suppressed and no where in history has there ever been a bloodless revolution.

America, recognize that your government does not have your best interests at heart….don't sit back like the Romans and let corruption and immorality become the norm. Don't depend upon the mainstream media to tell you what is going on…most are owned or controlled by those with the most to lose if the truth were reported. There are organizations you can join, like the American Freedom Campaign, to take an active role in turning back the tide of this nation's decline. Learn how to use the vast resources on the worldwide web to become informed, for an uninformed citizenry is powerless to effect change and change is what this country needs NOW!

All human beings are born free and equal in dignity and rights. They are endowed with reason and conscience and should act towards one another in the spirit of brotherhood."

Article 1, Universal Declaration of Human Rights,
United Nations, 1948

Recommended Reading

This list is provided so the reader can gain a more in-depth look at some of the topics presented for discussion in this book.

Global Research.ca
The Centre for Research on Globalization is an independent research organization and media group of writers, scholars, journalists and activists based in Montreal, CA. Through their website and books, they provide in-depth information and analysis on social, economic, and geopolitical issues that the mainstream media barely cover. Their name is also their website address.

Compromised: Clinton, Bush and the CIA by Terry Reid and John Cummings.

The Five Unanswered Questions About 9/11: What the 9/11 Commission Report Failed to Tell Us by James Ridgeway, Washington Correspondent for the *Village Voice*

9-11 by Noam Chomsky; Professor of Philosophy at the Massachusetts Institute of Technology

Are We Rome? The Fall of an Empire and the Fate of America by Cullen Murphey, Editor-at-large, *Vanity Fair*

The Revolution: A Manifesto by Dr. Ron Paul, former 2008 Presidential candidate.

End the Fed by Dr. Ron Paul.

China, Inc. by Ted C. Fishman (a compelling case for why America cannot afford to ignore the sleeping giant called China, the world's next superpower.)

The FairTax Book: Saying Goodbye to the Income Tax and the IRS by Neal Boortz and Congressman John Linder

Bailout Nation: How Greed and Easy Money Corrupted Wall Street and Shook the World by Barry Ritholtz with Aaron Task

The End of America: Letter of Warning to a Young Patriot by Naomi Wolf

The Dark Side: The Inside Story of How the War on Terror Turned into a War on American Ideals by Jane Mayer

Savage Inequalities by Jonathon Kozol

The Price of Loyalty by Ron Suskind

Bibliography

"Aboard a Slave Ship, 1829". Eyewitness to History. http:eyewitnesstohistory.com

911truth.org. *Insider Trading.* Cited from *Insider Trading Apparently Based on Foreknowledge of the 9/11 attacks.* (London Times, 9/11/2008) http://www.911truth.org

Bennett, William J. *Death of Outrage: Bill Clinton and the Assault on American Ideals.* (New York: Simon and Schuster, 1998)

Benson, Bill. http://www.thelawthatneverwas.com/new/home.asp

Black, Jim Nelson. *When Nations Die: America on the Brink; Ten Warning Signs of a Culture in Crisis.* (Illinois: Tyndale House Publishers, 1995)

Borger, Julian and Palast, Gregory. *Inquiry into new claims of poll abuses in Florida election.* The Guardian Unlimited, Feb 17, 2001 http://www.guardian.co.uk/world/2001/feb/17/usa.julianborger/

Carcopino, Jerome. *Daily Life in Ancient Rome: The People and the City at the Height of the Empire; Second Edition.* Edited and annotated by Henry T. Roswell. Yale University Press, 1968

CBS News. *Saddam's Ouster Planned in'01?* Posted 1/10/2004 on commondreams.org http://www.commondreams.org/headlines04/0110-03.htm

Citizens for Responsibility and Ethics in Washington (CREW). *CREW's Most Corrupt: Rep Ken Calvert* http://www.crewsmostcorrupt.org/summaries/calvert.php

Clinton Coke Lines. www.video.google.com Former CIA operative Gene Tatum, who defected from the CIA and disappeared shortly after this interview in 1998, tells of his first hand knowledge of Clinton's involvement in cocaine importing into the U.S. while governor of Arkansas (interviewed by Ted Gunderson, (ret.) FBI Senior Special Agent-in-Charge, Los Angeles

D'Amato, Paul. *U.S. Intervention in the Middle East: Blood for Oil*. International Socialist Review. Issue 15, December 2000-January 2001 Online Edition

Dadoo, Suraya. *When Uncle Sam Comes Calling in Africa*. Znet online magazine. Posted 4/30/2003 http://www.zmag.org/content/showarticle.ctm Retrieved 12/26/2006

DeRienzo, Paul. *Arkansas Governor Bill Clinton, President George (H.W.) Bush, CIA Drugs for Guns Connection*. N.C.O.I.C. Civil Intelligence Association, Defense Oversight Group http://www.ncoic.com/clinton.htm

Domhoff, William G. Who Rules America: *Wealth, Income and Power*. Retrieved from http://sociology.ucsc.edu/whorulesamerica/power/wealth.html

Engdahl, William F. *China and USA in New Cold War over Africa's Riches*. Global Research Posted May 20, 2007 http://globalresearch.ca/printarticle.php Retrieved 4/16/2008

FOXNEWS: *Porked: Earmarked for Profit*. Video broadcast 8/2008

Inaba, Ian (Director). *American Blackout*. (Video available on Vodpod.com) Produced by Guerilla News Network, 2006

Kennedy, Jr., Robert F. *Was the 2004 Election Stolen?* Rolling Stone Magazine, 6/1/06 http://www.rollingstone.com/news/story/10432334/was_the_2004_election_stolen

Lendman, Stephen. *The Federal Reserve*. Znet – The Spirit of Resistance Lives. Posted June 29, 2006. http://www.zmag.org/znet/viewarticle/3649

Liberty Tree.ca. Quotes by Josiah Stamp. http://quotes.liberty-tree.ca/quotes_by/sir+josiah+stamp

Lipscomb and Bergh, Editors. <u>The Writings of Thomas Jefferson</u> Memorial Edition, http://www. etext.virginia.edu

Miller, Jason. *American Capitalism and the Moral Poverty of Nations*. Posted 5/29/06 http://www.worldphilosophy.cn/html/haiwaishuping/200909/20-561.html

Motlagh, Jason. *America's AfricaCorps*. AsiaTimes Online 9/21/2006 http://www.atimes.com

Mount, Steve. *Events Affecting the Constitution: Scott vs. Sanford (60 U.S. 393) 1857* US Constitution.net Posted January 24, 2010 http://www.usconstitution.net/events.html

Murphey, Rhoads. *A Closer Look: Calcutta, Colonial Capital* .A History of Asia. Pg 302 Pearson Education, Inc. 2009

Mynott, Adam. *U.S. Africa Command Battles Skeptics*. Posted on BBC News 10/1/2008 http://newsvote.bbc.co.uk/mpapps/pagetools/print/news Retrieved 10/5/2008

National Center for Public Policy and Higher Education. *Measuring Up 2008*. http://measuring up2008.highereducation.org

Oramas, Joaquin. *Oil, the Only U.S. Interest in Africa*. Political Affairs Magazine Online Edition July – August 2005 http://politicalaffairs.net/article/view/1487/1/08

Ploch, Lauren. CRS Report RL34003. *Africa Command: U.S. Strategic Interests and the Role of the Military in Africa*. Congressional Research Service Issued December 7, 2007

Population Research Bureau (PRB). The 2010 Census Questionnaire: 7 Questions for Everyone. http://www.prb.org/Articles/2009/questionnaire.aspx

Public Education Center (PEC) Report. *Terrorist Plans to Use Planes as Weapons date to 1995: WTC Bomber Yousef confesses to*

U.S. Agents in 1995. Public Education Center, Washington, D.C. http://www.publicedcenter.org/faaterrorist.htm

Rogers, J.A. *The 5 Negro Presidents.* Helga M. Rogers, St. Petersburg, FL 1965

Rosenfeld, Steven. *In Violation of Federal Law, Ohio's 2004 Presidential Election Records Are Destroyed or Missing.* Alternet. org, July 30, 2007. http://www.alternet.org/story/58328

Schneider, Patricia. Case Teaching Notes for "The Case of Desiree's Baby: The Genetics and Evolution of Skin Color." Queensborough Community College, Bayside, NY from the case studies of The National Center for Case Study in Teaching Science, 2003 http://www.sciencecases.org/skin_color/skin_ color_notes.asp

US Bureau of Labor Statistics. *Work Experience Summary.* December 8, 2009 http://www.bls.gov/news.release/work. nr0.htm

US Census Bureau News. *U.S. Hispanic Population Surpasses 45 Million; Now 15% of Total* Released May 1, 2008 http:www.census.gov/pressrelease/www/releases/archives/ population/011910.htm

Whitman, David. *When Work Disappears: The World of the New Urban Poor.* Washington Monthly, 11/1996

Woodson, Carter G. *The Mis-education of the Negro.* Associated Publishers, 1933 Reprinted by Africa World Press, Inc. Trenton, NJ, 1990

www.ingramcontent.com/pod-product-compliance
Lightning Source LLC
Chambersburg PA
CBHW020306290526
45784CB00003B/1377